THE WORLD-CLASS
WEALTH
MINDSET

THE WORLD-CLASS
WEALTH
MINDSET

Four Pillars to Building
Personal Freedom

ARASH VOSSOUGHI

Foreword by Mykie Stiller

Published 2024 by Gildan Media LLC
aka G&D Media
www.GandDmedia.com

Front cover design by Amber Reed

Interior design by Meghan Day Healey of Story Horse, LLC

Library of Congress Cataloging-in-Publication Data is available upon request

ISBN: 978-1-7225-0680-3

10   9   8   7   6   5   4   3   2   1

To my wife, Veronica,
and our amazing kids, Andre and Maya:
this book is a tribute to you,
the guiding stars of my life's work.

Contents

PART ONE

The World-Class Wealth Mindset

PART TWO

The World-Class Wealth Mindset in Action

PART THREE

Raising the Global Standard

APPENDIX

Worksheets and Quizzes

Acknowledgments

There are many people I owe thanks and gratitude to on my journey from failing significantly to achieving world-class wealth—a few of which I must mention in this book.

My greatest mentor and dearest friend Bob Proctor, there are not enough words to express my gratitude for the impact you had on my life.

My mom, Shay, I wouldn't be who I am without you. You modeled true strength and always believed in me.

My brother, Bobby, your unwavering support in my life means that absolute world to me and has given me more strength than you realize.

My business partner and friend, Mykie. We've been working together for fifteen years and we're just getting started.

Our entire team at Voss Coaching Co, especially Monica and Nicole.

Foreword

We've all heard that success isn't a destination, it's a journey. But what does "success" really mean? Many people think that it is measured in terms of financial wealth. Although that's part of it, I believe you can't have *true* wealth and rich experiences without holistic wealth—wealth in your mind, wealth in your health, wealth in your relationships, and yes—wealth in your bank account.

Wealth is a journey that requires the right mindset and relentless discipline. It doesn't just happen: it's something we need to cultivate and act upon every single day. That's why this book was written.

My name is Mykie Stiller, and introducing you to the pages of *The World-Class Wealth Mindset* is an absolute privilege.

For more than fifteen years, I have had the joy of walking alongside my dear friend and business partner, Arash Vossoughi. We've navigated through challenges that have tested our resolve and celebrated victories that have inspired us to reach even greater heights. Since I first met him, one thing has remained constant: his unwavering commitment to helping YOU.

Arash's life's mission is to arm people with the information to change their lives, infuse them with the belief that anything is possible, and give them specific step-by-step instructions to help them live a life of freedom—consistently and in the long term.

The World-Class Wealth Mindset is not just a book: it's a guide to the mindset that distinguishes those who are winning in life from those who are missing the mark.

As you turn these pages, your beliefs will be challenged, you will experience mindset shifts, acquire new daily disciplines, and understand perspectives that Arash has honed and refined over the years. He started as a dedicated student, applied what he discovered, and is now one of the world's leading mentors.

This isn't just theory. It is a practical guide that draws from real-life experiences, real-life challenges, and real-life successes and gives you very applicable practical direction.

Arash is not your typical author, and this is not your typical book. Arash's approach breathes a fresh perspective rooted in authenticity, empathy, and a deep understanding of human behavior. He doesn't just offer mindsets and strategies; he offers insights that resonate on a personal level, challenging you to question your assumptions, redefine your goals, and ultimately live a life of freedom.

Through these pages, you'll discover the importance of a mindset that doesn't accept excuses or circumstances but instead embraces abundance and freedom. Arash invites you to break free from limitations, redefine your relationship with wealth, and embrace a world-class mindset that extends beyond monetary gain, encompassing fulfillment and purpose.

As you dive in, remember that you hold in your hands more than just a book. You hold the map to wealth and success, guided by the insights of a true practitioner and one of the world's leading mindset mentors. May this journey inspire you, empower you, and propel you toward a world-class wealth mindset beyond what you thought was possible.

—Mykie Stiller
CEO and cofounder
Voss Coaching Co.

Introduction

You are ready. This is the first page of the book that can and will change your entire life. In fact, close your eyes right now and lock this feeling in . . . the anticipation and excitement and the knowledge that you've found the key to unlock your dreams. This is it—the day your mindset begins to change in ways that will soon affect your wealth and every other aspect of your life.

You might be thinking, "Arash, that's a pretty bold statement." And it is. But I have seen this shift happen thousands of times, and I know it can happen for you.

Let's start with a question: who is the most important person in the world? The first answer that comes to your mind might be a family member, such as your partner or children. Or you might think of a friend or mentor. But the true answer is *you*. You are the most important person in your world.

Your Mind Determines How You See the World

The way you perceive the world is directly influenced by the internal landscape of your mind. It's not a statement made with ego or arrogance, but rather a simple fact. Your self-perception, the thoughts you focus on, the way you spend your time, and other aspects of your life shape your perspective. Ultimately, nobody cares about you and your life more than you do. From your own individual standpoint, you are the most important person in your world.

The way we perceive the world is a blend of our external experiences and the internal landscape of our minds. Our self-perception, thoughts, actions, and the choices we make all contribute to shaping our unique perspective on reality. Some people may mistakenly believe that this statement means that we are being self-centered or arrogant. It's not! It just means that the way we see ourselves, the standards we hold for ourselves, our attitude, and the level of discipline we have all come from living life inside out.

Our self-perception, or how we see ourselves, plays a pivotal role in shaping our outlook on the world. It encompasses our beliefs, values, strengths, weaknesses, and the narrative we construct about our own identity. The lens through which we view ourselves acts as a filter, influencing how we interpret and respond to the events and circumstances we encounter. A positive self-perception can fill us with confidence, resilience, and a sense of purpose, while a negative self-perception can hinder our growth, dampen our spirit, and limit our potential.

Where We Put Our Attention Is What Grows

The thoughts we choose to focus on affect our perception of reality. Our minds are constantly generating a stream of thoughts, and the ones we give attention to shape our experiences. When we direct our thoughts towards gratitude, possibilities, and growth, we invite a more optimistic and expansive perspective. Dwelling on negative thoughts, self-doubt, and limitations can cloud our perception, creating a narrower view of the world and limiting our ability to seize opportunities.

The way we spend our time also contributes to the shaping of our perception. Our daily habits, routines, and activities influence the information we consume, the people we interact with, and the experiences we accumulate. Engaging in activities that align with our passions, values, and aspirations give us perspective, providing us with a greater sense of fulfillment and purpose. Investing time in negative or unproductive pursuits can distort our perception, leading to dissatisfaction, disillusionment, and a limited view of what is possible.

Empathy Still Matters

Even though each of us is the most important person in our own lives, this doesn't mean that we don't care about other people. The world is filled with all kinds of diversity and differences, and our freedom comes from developing connections with all kinds of people.

Recognizing that we are the primary caretakers of our own lives empowers us to prioritize our well-being, make choices that align with our values, and take charge of our own happiness and growth. It emphasizes the significance of self-care and self-responsibility.

From our individual standpoints, each of us is indeed the most important person in our world. This perspective does not diminish the value of others or negate the importance of relationships, but rather highlights the necessity of self-love, self-acceptance, and self-advocacy. When we prioritize our own well-being and personal growth, we enhance our capacity to positively affect the lives of those around us, creating a ripple effect of compassion, inspiration, and meaningful connections.

In short, the way we perceive the world comes directly from the internal landscape of our minds. Our self-perception, the thoughts we focus on, how we spend our time, and other factors shape our unique perspective. Recognizing that nobody cares about our lives more than we do empowers us to prioritize our own well-being, make intentional choices, and cultivate a positive mindset. By understanding the influence of our internal landscape, we can navigate life with greater self-awareness, compassion, and purpose, ultimately leading to a more fulfilling and enriched existence.

I Like Me!

The degree to which you like and respect yourself, along with your self-image, plays a crucial role in determining various aspects of your life. They have a significant impact on your happiness, well-being, self-confidence, and financial prosperity. Your self-image also influences the goals you set for yourself and how you navigate obstacles that come your way. Furthermore, it shapes your interactions with other people and determines the level of consistency and persistence you exhibit in pursuing what truly matters to you.

When you have a positive self-image and hold yourself to high standards, you are more likely to experience greater happiness and fulfillment. This self-assuredness empowers you to overcome challenges and setbacks, because you believe in your ability to overcome them. It fuels your self-confidence and enables you to take risks and seize opportunities, ultimately contributing to your personal and professional growth.

Conversely, a negative self-image can hinder your progress and limit your potential. It can undermine your self-confidence, making it difficult for you to assert yourself or pursue your goals with conviction. It may lead to self-doubt and a lack of belief in your capabilities, hindering your ability to take necessary actions and seize opportunities for growth.

Mindset Matters

Cultivating a World-Class Mindset is vital for personal development and achieving freedom in every aspect of life. By recognizing your worth, setting standards, having the right attitude, and engaging in the discipline and actions that align with your values and aspirations, you can create a foundation for greater happiness, confidence, and success.

Recognize Your Worth

Recognizing your worth is an essential starting point. You possess inherent value and deserve to be treated with respect and dignity. However, self-worth is not merely a concept to understand intellectually; it must be deeply internalized and genuinely believed. It involves acknowledging one's strengths, embracing imperfections, and fostering self-compassion. Recognizing and appreciating your worth makes it easier to set healthy boundaries, make empowered choices, and pursue endeavors that align with personal values and aspirations.

You are worth the effort!

Raise Your Standard

Setting standards is an essential pillar in the journey of personal freedom and cultivating a World-Class Mindset. Standards act as a compass, guiding us towards excellence, integrity, and authenticity in every aspect of our lives. They reflect values and aspirations and shape our daily decisions and actions.

When we set high standards for ourselves, we create a framework for success and fulfillment. These standards provide a clear vision of what we want to achieve and how we want to show up in the world. Whether it's in personal relationships, career, health, or personal growth, these standards become the yardstick against which we measure our progress. They ensure that we will consistently refuse to settle for less than we deserve.

By holding ourselves accountable to these standards, we take ownership of our lives. We recognize that they have the power to shape our own destiny and make choices that align with our values and goals. This sense of personal responsibility fuels motivation and a drive for continuous improvement. It encourages us to go above and beyond, pushing the boundaries of what we thought was possible.

Standards Affect Self-Image

Setting standards also fosters self-respect and raises your self-esteem. When you hold yourself to a high Standard of conduct and achievement and then follow through with action, you develop a deep sense of self-worth. You understand and prove to yourself that you deserve the best that life has to offer and are willing to put in the effort and dedication required to reach your full potential.

Standards serve as a powerful tool for self-reflection and growth. They provide a benchmark for assessing your progress and identifying areas for development. When we fall short of our standards, we can either feel bad about ourselves and start to wonder if we are a loser or are destined to fail. A better approach is to view apparent failure as an opportunity for learning and growth. Failure and setbacks are stepping stones to propel us forward, so that we are constantly striving to raise the bar and surpass our previous achievements.

Setting high standards is a fundamental aspect of cultivating a World-Class Mindset. It empowers us to define our own path, embrace personal responsibility, and continually push ourselves toward excellence. By setting clear expectations and holding ourselves accountable, we lay the foundation for a fulfilling and successful life.

Your Attitude Determines Your Altitude

Maintaining the right attitude is not just a passive state of mind; it is an active and powerful tool for shaping and nurturing a resilient and growth-oriented mindset. It goes beyond mere positivity and involves a conscious and deliberate choice to adopt thoughts and perspectives that support personal growth and well-being. As we'll see later, the thoughts you choose to accept enter directly into your subconscious mind affect every area of your life.

A positive attitude serves as a guiding light during challenging times, helping you navigate through obstacles, setbacks, and uncertainties with grace and determination. Instead of viewing setbacks as insurmountable roadblocks, a positive attitude enables you to reframe them as valuable opportunities for learning, growth, and self-improvement. It allows you to extract valuable lessons from each experience and use them to fuel your personal development journey.

Embracing optimism is crucial for maintaining the right attitude. It means choosing to see the world through a lens of possibility and hope, even in the face of adversity. Optimism encourages you to focus on solutions rather than dwelling on problems, empowering you to approach challenges with a proactive and solutions-oriented mindset. It enables you to believe in your own capabilities and the potential for positive outcomes.

Cultivating gratitude is another integral aspect of maintaining the right attitude. It involves consciously recognizing and appreciating the blessings, joys, and positive aspects of your life, no matter how small. Practicing gratitude shifts your focus from what is lacking to what is present, fostering contentment and abundance. It cultivates a mindset of appreciation and allows you to find joy and fulfillment in the present moment, enhancing your well-being.

Nurturing a positive attitude enhances your capacity to overcome obstacles and persist in the face of challenges. It keeps you motivated and energized, fueling your drive to pursue your goals and dreams. Additionally, a positive attitude has a ripple effect on your experiences and relationships. It attracts positive people, opportunities, and experiences into your life, creating a virtuous cycle of growth and success.

Maintaining the right attitude is an intentional and powerful practice that shapes your mindset and ultimately determines the trajectory of your life. By consciously choosing positive thoughts, reframing setbacks, embracing optimism, and cultivating gratitude, you empower yourself to overcome challenges, stay motivated, and attract positivity into your life. Embrace the power of a positive attitude, and witness the transformative impact it can have on your personal growth and well-being.

Discipline Is Freedom

Cultivating a World-Class Mindset goes beyond Attitude and entails disciplined actions that align with your values and aspirations. While Attitude sets the foundation for your mindset, disciplined actions enable you to bring your intentions to life and create tangible progress towards your desired outcomes.

Discipline is the bridge between setting goals and achieving them. It involves consistently taking intentional steps and making conscious choices that propel you towards your aspirations, even in the face of obstacles, challenges, or distractions. It requires unwavering focus, commitment, and perseverance.

Discipline is the bridge between setting goals and achieving them.

When you align your actions with your values, you reinforce your sense of purpose and integrity. You uphold the principles and beliefs that guide you, fostering a strong sense of self and identity. By consistently acting in accordance with your values, you cultivate a deep sense of authenticity and congruence within yourself.

Disciplined actions also boost self-confidence. Each time you follow through on your commitments, overcome resistance, and stay dedicated to your path, you build trust and belief in your abilities. The act of consistently showing up for yourself and taking steps towards your goals reinforces your sense of efficacy and strengthens your belief in what you can achieve.

Discipline powerfully propels you toward your goals. It helps you overcome the temptations of instant gratification or short-term distractions. By consistently acting in alignment with your values and aspirations, you create positive momentum and progress.

Discipline also serves as a guiding principle that helps you make deliberate choices. It provides a framework for decision-making, allowing you to prioritize what truly matters, and say no to distractions or activities that do not align with your goals. Through discipline, you gain clarity and create a sense of structure in your life, optimizing your time and energy for what truly matters to you.

Discipline empowers you to consistently take intentional steps towards your desired outcomes, reinforcing your sense of purpose, integrity, and self-confidence. By aligning your actions with your values, you strengthen your commitment to personal growth and propel yourself closer to your goals. Embrace discipline as a powerful tool in your journey towards a World-Class Mindset and a fulfilling life.

The World-Class Mindset Is Not a Destination

Personal development and success are not static destinations but ongoing journeys. You have to constantly reassess and refine your mindset and actions. This can involve learning new things, developing new skills, getting help from a mentor or coach, and embracing personal growth opportunities. By continually investing in self-improvement, you expand your capabilities, broaden your perspectives, and unlock new possibilities for success.

Remember, you are the protagonist of your own life story. How you perceive yourself, value yourself, and cultivate your mindset profoundly impacts the quality of your life and the fulfillment you experience. Embrace the power within you to shape your self-image and steer your life in a direction that aligns with your true desires and aspirations.

Your mindset is the defining statement about you and the quality of your life.

Who Am I?

Who am I as the author of this book, and how do I know these things? I am the cofounder of Voss Coaching Co. and have more than fifteen years in the personal development industry. With experience in sales, marketing, and business, my company has helped hundreds of thousands of people, spread across two dozen countries, break through barriers and get what they really want in their lives.

I am committed to you and your success, and that's why I wrote this book. Although I travel the world speaking and sharing these ideas, I wanted to make sure that these ideas get out to as many people as possible. After all, everyone wants a better life. And I understand that everyone *can* change their mindset to get the life they want and deserve.

Does that mean that it will be easy? Yes and no. The ideas presented in this book have been around for centuries, and once you start to use them, wealth and abundance will begin to flow into your life with shocking ease and speed. But it can be hard to challenge your core beliefs and attitudes. It can be difficult to rewrite the program of your conscious mind and rebuild your mindset from the foundation up.

If you follow exactly what I tell you in this book, do the exercises and the work, and apply these ideas to your life every day, you can do it. It's time to bet on yourself and know, without a doubt, that you can develop the mindset of wealth and that it will show up in ways you can't even imagine right now.

The Structure of the Book

This book is divided into three parts. Part 1 is where you'll discover how your mind really works and learn the tools to develop a world class wealth mindset. Then, in part 2, you'll start to apply the four pillars of success to your everyday life. In doing this, you'll see your wealth grow and your life improve. Finally, in part 3, you'll start to pay it forward. By then, the people in your life will be noticing the difference, and you'll learn how to deepen the roots of the four pillars and help others grow into their own abundance.

I have discovered that there are four pillars of success, and the book is structured around them. In each chapter, I go into great detail about one of the pillars and have created exercises and worksheets to help you lock down the ideas and put them into practice. The four pillars are *Image*, *Standard*, *Attitude*, and *Discipline*.

The
Four Pillars of Success

Image Standard Attitude Discipline

Throughout the book, you'll see icons that identify different types of content.

 The lock represents a core idea that you want to lock in.

 The question mark highlights a brief quiz to make sure you're understanding the material.

 The pencil indicates that you're to fill out a worksheet in the book's appendix.

 The barbell illustrates an exercise that you'll do in the real world to help you apply the ideas you're learning throughout. Taken together, these actions will solidify the foundation that supports the four pillars.

The Most Important Part of the Book

If you're like most people, you may want to skip ahead of all the background and mindset stuff and get to the "action" part. In our society, we're conditioned that "doing" creates success. In one sense, it's true. You're not going to grow your wealth by sitting on the couch meditating on the ideas. Action is certainly necessary. But, it's not the most important part.

The most important part of the book isn't in your hands. It's between your ears. As you proceed through the book, you'll get the most benefit from it if you continually think about the ideas presented here. The more you shift your thoughts, the more opportunities will come your way to take meaningful action. Read each chapter more than once. When you are in the car or on the subway or train, look at your world differently. Start to notice how your life is on an upward spiral of ever-increasing success and achievement.

One Day or Day One?

Are you going to do this one day, or is this day one of your new mindset? Right now, make an irrevocable decision that nothing outside of you controls your thinking. This is a line in the sand that can never be uncrossed. Commit that you are willing to pay the price to get the life you want.

Fill out the Four-Pillar Pledge, and make that commitment before going on in the book.

◄▬▬▮ At this point, please go to the appendix at the back of this book and fill out worksheet 1: the Four-Pillar Pledge.

Are you ready to develop the World-Class Wealth Mindset? Let's go.

PART ONE

The World-Class Wealth Mindset

1

You Are Designed for Greatness

Liz* sat in her car, with tears streaming down her face that matched the rain running down her car windows. "How can this still be happening?" she asked no one in particular. It was two days before Christmas, and she was sitting in the parking lot of Target with a small but important list of items to get. These were not extravagances, but were things like dog food and dry pasta and sauce for her family's "Christmas dinner." "I may be broke, but I know how to stretch a dollar," she would often say. But on this day, after having spent an hour inside of Target carefully selecting the most inexpensive items so that she could pull off Christmas for her family, her credit card had been declined, she didn't have enough cash in the bank, and there was no one she could call to help pay for the items. She walked out of Target with empty hands and a heart full of shame. "What am I going to do?"

Every single person reading this book has something in their past to which they can relate this story. We've all had tough times and challenges to overcome. Some of us have had profoundly difficult life experiences that seem impossible to rise above. It's tempting to look at those who have succeeded and think, "Well, sure, If I'd had the advantages they had, I'd be wealthy too."

---

* The people mentioned in the book are composites of different clients I've had over the years. The stories are the same, but the details have been changed.

This is a flawed mindset that has kept you from the level of success you want.

> Everything you think and do, or fail to think and do, has an effect somewhere in your life.

Everything we think, do, or fail to think and do has an impact on our lives. Our thoughts, beliefs, and actions shape our experiences, relationships, and overall well-being. Each decision we make, no matter how small, can ripple through different areas of our life and influence the outcomes we encounter.

Thought: The Most Potent Form of Suggestion

Our thoughts play a significant role in shaping our perception of the world and ourselves. They can either empower us or hold us back. Positive and empowering thoughts can instill confidence, motivation, and resilience, while negative or limiting thoughts can create self-doubt, fear, and limitations. The way we think about ourselves and the world around us influences our attitudes, choices, and behaviors, ultimately affecting the outcomes we achieve.

Similarly, our actions are the manifestation of our thoughts and beliefs. Each action we take carries the potential to bring us closer to our goals or move us further away from them. Consistent, purposeful actions aligned with our values and aspirations can lead to progress, growth, and success. On the other hand, neglecting to take action or engaging in actions that contradict our values can hinder our personal development and impede our desired outcomes.

The actions we choose *not* to take can also have consequences. Procrastination, for instance, can delay progress and create missed opportunities. Failure to address important matters or make necessary changes in our lives can lead to us getting stuck and being dissatisfied. Even inaction has an effect, so we have to take responsibility for our thoughts: they lead to the choices that determine the direction of our lives.

Our thoughts and actions affect not only us but also the people around us. We all know what it's like to be around someone who has a negative attitude and low standards for themselves and doesn't have the discipline to do what they say they're going to do. It brings us down!

Research shows that we are influenced most by the five closest people to us. Are you raising everyone up? You can make other people better—or worse—by your thoughts and attitude.

The energy we radiate, the attitudes we adopt, and the behaviors we exhibit can influence the dynamics of our relationships, both personal and professional. Positive and supportive interactions can foster harmony, trust, and collaboration, while negative or harmful behaviors can damage relationships and hinder progress.

> Success is the result of small disciplines compounded over time.

If you want to know what you have been thinking, take a look at your current results. Sometimes the effects of our thoughts aren't immediately obvious. But when you stop and look around at the results in your life, you can see what you've been thinking. If you're experiencing lack and limitation in any area of your life, then that's an area where your thoughts aren't in alignment with your goals. We have to be constantly on guard to watch what we are thinking and keep changing it to resonate with the vibration of our goals.

Everything we think and do, or fail to think and do, has consequences in our lives. Our thoughts shape our attitudes, beliefs, and perceptions, while our actions manifest our intentions and determine our outcomes. By cultivating positive thoughts, taking intentional actions, and embracing personal responsibility, we can have a positive impact on ourselves and those around us. Recognizing the power of our thoughts and actions empowers us to create the life we desire and contribute to the well-being of our communities and the world at large.

Every Result Has a Corresponding Cause

It's easy to see cause and effect in the physical world. If you don't clean your home or your car, it gets dirty. If you make it a practice to regularly clean these items, they stay clean. Cause—effect. If you sit on your rear end, eat chips, and watch television every day instead of making healthy lifestyle choices, your body won't look or feel its best. If you eat healthy foods, move your body, and drink water, your body will look and feel better.

When it comes to something less tangible, like wealth, the direct relation of cause and effect can be harder to see. But it's there all the same. Thoughts are causes, and conditions are effects. You are creating your life every minute of every day by the way you think about yourself and your world.

Thoughts are indeed the causes, and conditions are the effects in our lives. Our thoughts shape our beliefs, attitudes, and perceptions, which in turn influence our actions, decisions, and experiences. The way we think about ourselves and the world around us plays a fundamental role in creating our reality.

When we consistently entertain positive and empowering thoughts, we cultivate a mindset that is conducive to personal growth, happiness, and success. Positive thoughts can generate feelings of optimism, self-confidence, and resilience, leading us to take actions aligned with our goals and aspirations. As a result, we create favorable conditions and attract opportunities that support our desired outcomes.

On the other hand, if our thoughts are predominantly negative, self-limiting, or filled with doubt and fear, we tend to create conditions that reflect those beliefs. Negative thoughts can generate feelings of anxiety and self-doubt, which may lead to self-sabotaging behaviors or missed opportunities. The conditions we experience in our lives often mirror the quality of our thoughts and the mindset we cultivate.

Choose Your Thoughts, Choose Your Future

We have the power to consciously choose our thoughts and shape our mindset. By developing self-awareness and mindfulness, we can observe our thoughts and challenge any negative or limiting beliefs that arise. Through introspection and self-reflection, we can reframe negative thoughts, replace them with positive and empowering ones, and consciously direct our thinking towards what we truly desire.

While external circumstances and events may be beyond our control, we can control our responses to them and the meaning we assign to them. By consciously choosing positive thoughts and interpretations, even in challenging situations, we can shift our perspective and create a more empowering narrative for ourselves. This in turn influences our emotional state and actions, and the outcomes we experience.

Creating our lives through thoughts does not mean that we have complete control over every external circumstance or outcome. Life is complex, and various factors beyond our thoughts and actions can come into play. However, by recognizing the power of our thoughts and taking responsibility for our mindset, we can significantly influence our responses to external events and create a more positive and fulfilling life.

By understanding that our thoughts are the causes and conditions are the effects, we become conscious cocreators of our reality. We have the ability to shape our lives and manifest our desires by consciously choosing thoughts that align with our values, goals, and aspirations. Embracing the power of our thoughts empowers us to take ownership of our lives and create a future that is aligned with our highest potential.

Create Your Future, Don't Recreate Your Past

Similarly, the way you perceive and interpret your past experiences has a profound impact on how you approach your present life. Our past experiences shape our beliefs, attitudes, and expectations, influencing our thoughts, emotions, and behaviors in the present.

Holding on to negative or limiting beliefs about your past can cloud your perception of the present and hinder your ability to embrace and enjoy your current circumstances. If you constantly dwell on past mistakes, failures, or disappointments, it can create a negative mindset that colors your perspective and prevents you from seeing possibilities and opportunities in the present. Moreover, it recreates those same experiences again and again in your present life.

On the other hand, when you choose to reframe your past experiences in a positive and empowering light, it can have a transformative effect on your present life. By focusing on the lessons learned, the growth achieved, and the resilience developed through challenging times, you cultivate a mindset of gratitude, resilience, and optimism. This perspective allows you to appreciate the journey that has led you to where you are today and instills confidence in your ability to overcome future obstacles.

Viewing your past experiences as valuable learning opportunities rather than as failures enables you to extract wisdom and insights that can guide your present decisions and actions. It empowers you to make conscious choices based on your newfound understanding, helping you navigate challenges and pursue goals with greater clarity and intention.

By consciously shaping your thoughts and beliefs about the past, you have the power to transform your present reality. Instead of being weighed down by regrets or dwelling on negative experiences, you can focus on the positive aspects, the growth you've experienced, and the strength you've gained. This mindset shift allows you to approach your present life with optimism, resilience, and a sense of possibility.

By reframing your past in a positive light and extracting the valuable lessons it holds, you empower yourself to embrace the present moment, make the most of your current circumstances, and create a future filled with growth, fulfillment, and joy.

The Movie Analogy

What's your favorite movie? (You know, the one you can see over and over again and practically memorized.) Close your eyes and recall a scene from that movie right now. Really get into the scene and feel how thrilling or sad or happy watching the movie makes you feel. (Don't just keep reading—really do it!)

OK, now think of an event from your past. Don't pick something really traumatic (like when your dad left home when you were five years old and never came back). Choose something rather mundane, like the time your favorite sports team won the championship. Go ahead and close your eyes and recall that memory with vivid detail. Relive it fully.

Now that you've done that, ask yourself, "What's the difference between the two visualizations?" As you sat there in this present moment and recalled seeing the movie scene and living the past event, what was the difference?

The answer? Nothing. There was no difference at all between remembering a scene from a movie and recalling a scene from your past. They both exist only in your mind now.

This is a mind-blowing realization, isn't it? All of those stories that you keep telling yourself about your past and how this or that held you back from greatness are false. You only keep them alive in the retelling of them. Every time you waste one precious minute of mental energy thinking about the negative events in your past you are bringing it back to life and bringing it into your present experience.

Instead, let's spend some time reframing those experiences so that you can see them for the gifts they are. Just as in a movie when the character experiences the "all is lost" moment, your past has prepared you for greatness.

🔒 You Are Designed for Greatness

Liz, in our opening scenario, was experiencing her "all is lost" moment. Years later, she kept telling that story as an example of how bad her marriage was at the time and how unfair her life had been. We coached her on how to reframe that experience and see it as the point in which things began to change for her. It was a key part of her hero's journey. She learned to stop telling that story and reliving it in her mind over and over again, and instead became grateful for the catalyst that it was. If she does share the story today, it's with a different tone and meaning. Liz no longer looks back at that event as something bad, but as something that prepared her for greatness.

What about you? How can you reframe the experiences from your past and discover the ways your past has prepared you for greatness? By practicing the art of neutrality.

The Art of Neutrality

The art of neutrality is the ability to look at your past in a neutral way, as if it were a scene from a movie or a book or an event that happened to someone else. Soon, we'll ask you to recall some events from your past and gain the understanding and perspective from those experiences.

Here's how the art of neutrality works. When Liz looks back on that day in the car outside of Target, she doesn't get sucked into the emotions and feelings of the day. She plays it like a movie, seeing herself from the outside. She sees the car and the rain and the windshield wipers. She sees a woman (herself) in the car crying. Then she asks, "What about this experience was a gift? How did this experience shift my thinking, which shifted my behavior?"

When we reflect on our past, we have the benefit of perspective. The saying "hindsight is 20/20" means that when we look back on the events and actions in our past, we have a much better idea of what we might have done differently, because we can see how it turned out.

The Farmer and the Horse

Here's a great ancient story that illustrates this concept. Many years ago, there was a farmer who lived on a simple ranch with his wife, his young son, and a workhorse. One day the son failed to close the barn door properly, and the horse ran away. The farmer's neighbors, hearing this news, came over to the farmer's house and lamented, "How awful for you! Your horse ran away. Who will help you pull the cart and work on the ranch? This is terrible."

The farmer simply replied, "Could be."

A few days later, the farmer and his wife were sitting on the porch drinking some lemonade when they heard sounds coming from over the hill. It sounded like hooves! Suddenly, the farmer saw his horse running toward the ranch, along with a dozen wild stallions. He jumped to his feet, called out for his son, and they wrangled the horses into the barn. The neighbors, upon hearing this, rushed over to him and said, "How wonderful! You are a wealthy man now! You can train and sell these horses and use the money to grow your ranch. This is a wonderful thing."

The farmer simply replied, "Could be."

Later that night, the farmer's son, who felt bad about leaving the gate open before, decided he was going to train the horses. He went out and attempted to mount the largest stallion. The horse threw him, and he broke both of his legs. When the neighbors heard of this, they ran over and talked to the farmer: "What a tragedy! Your son broke both of his legs, and it will take months for him to recover and be able to help you again. This is a terrible thing!"

The farmer simply replied, "Could be."

A few weeks later, war broke out in the country, and the young men and women in the village were called to enlist. They all died in a terrible explosion, leaving their parents devastated. At the town funeral service, the neighbors said to the farmer, "You are so lucky. If that horse hadn't thrown your son, he wouldn't have broken his legs, and he'd have been killed in the war too."

The farmer simply replied, "Could be."

Every event that happens in your life is neither good nor bad. It just *is*. It's how we perceive things that adds meaning. Events in themselves are neutral and do not inherently possess a positive or negative value. Our perception and interpretation of those events assign meaning and determine how we respond to them. Our subjective lens, shaped by our beliefs, experiences, and mindset, influences the way we perceive and make sense of the world around us.

Two people can experience the same event and have completely different reactions. For example, losing a job can be seen as a devastating setback by one person, while another may view it as an opportunity for growth and a chance to pursue a new career path. The event itself remains the same, but the meaning and emotional response vary greatly.

Our perceptions are influenced by a multitude of factors, including our beliefs, values, cultural background, past experiences, and personal biases. These factors shape our cognitive filters, which selectively interpret and process information. As a result, we may perceive events through a positive or negative lens, which can impact our emotions, thoughts, and subsequent actions.

Recognizing that our perceptions add meaning to events can be empowering. It means that we can consciously choose how we interpret and respond to our life circumstances. By cultivating a mindset that is open, flexible, and resilient, we can develop a more balanced and constructive perspective.

While it may not always be easy to adopt a positive outlook, especially in challenging situations, we can train ourselves to reframe our perceptions and find empowering meanings. This involves questioning our initial interpretations, challenging negative beliefs or assumptions, and seeking alternative perspectives. By doing so, we expand our perception and open ourselves up to new possibilities and solutions.

Practicing mindfulness and cultivating present-moment awareness can help us detach from automatic judgments and reactions. By observing our thoughts and emotions without immediate identification, we create space for more objective and conscious interpretations. This enables us to respond to events with greater clarity, wisdom, and resilience.

Perceiving events in a more neutral or positive light does not imply denying or dismissing the existence of challenges, pain, or suffering. It is merely an acknowledgment that our interpretations shape our emotional experiences and actions. By consciously choosing empowering meanings, we can navigate difficult circumstances with greater strength, resilience, and growth.

Because events in our lives are inherently neutral, it is our perceptions and interpretations that assign meaning. By cultivating self-awareness, challenging limiting beliefs, and adopting a mindset that is open to alternative perspectives, we can shape our interpretations and responses to events. Embracing the understanding that events just *are* allows us to approach life with greater flexibility, resilience, and transformative potential.

Use this insight to reflect on how the so-called negative experiences of your life actually led to something good, or they were just neutral events: nothing more and nothing less.

◄▬▬▌ Before going on in the book, go to the appendix and complete worksheet 2 to learn how your past has prepared you for greatness.

In the next chapter, we'll discover how your mind really works so that we can use it to reprogram your mindset.

2

How Your Mind Works

Chris is a thirty-five-year-old artist who has been apprenticing under a temperamental sculptor named John. Ever since Chris was a teenager, he's been painting and drawing but has discovered that creating bronze sculptures is his favorite form of artistic expression, which is why he took the apprenticeship with the famously difficult artist. Unfortunately, Chris's dad is an engineer at the department of water and power and doesn't approve of his son's interest in the arts. Between his dad's lack of support and John's intense critique, it has been a challenge for Chris to stay positive about his potential success as an artist. Nevertheless, he continues to sculpt and approach gallery owners about having his pieces displayed. Rejection after rejection only serve to confirm what his dad and John have been telling him: he isn't good enough. "What am I doing wrong?" he wonders. "I know I have talent. Why can't I get someone else to see it?"

Have you ever wondered where your mind is located? We all know where our physical brains are, of course. But where in the brain does the conscious mind exist?

Scientists have been unable to locate one specific place in the brain where the conscious mind can be found. Instead, it's thought to be a combination of sensory input from the various places of the brain that filters through the prefrontal cortex to create thought. As a result, what we observe in the external world is heavily individual.

Two people can be in the same environment and experience the same events, sights, sounds, smells, and tastes, but can come away with completely different interpretations of what happened.

This occurs because our conscious mind is influenced by things other than what our senses tell us. For example, you and I can go out to eat, and for dessert we might have apple pie and ice cream. If you have a positive memory associated with that dessert because it reminds you of Sunday dinners with your grandmother, your conscious mind will perceive it as a good experience. Maybe I don't have that experience, because I didn't grow up with apple pie and ice cream. It's a good enough dessert, but doesn't evoke the same emotions and experience that it does in you. Let's say, also, that the person at the next table is also eating apple pie with ice cream, but she feels guilty pleasure because she was overweight as a child, and her mother told her not to have dessert. All of us are having the same sensory experience: eating apple pie with ice cream. But we are each having different conscious experiences (positive, neutral, negative) based on nothing that is happening in the moment. How can that be? How can we all observe the same thing and have vastly different experiences? Here are some reasons.

Subjectivity of perception. Perception is a subjective process. Our senses receive raw sensory information from the external world, but our brains actively interpret and make sense of that information based on our unique cognitive filters, past experiences, beliefs, and biases. Consequently, two people can perceive the same event differently, focusing on different details or aspects based on their own perceptual biases.

Cognitive and emotional filters. Cognitive and emotional filters play a crucial role in shaping our experiences. These filters are formed by our beliefs, values, cultural backgrounds, personal experiences, and even our current mood or state of mind. They act as lenses through which we filter incoming information, selectively attending to certain aspects and disregarding others. As a result, you may focus on different elements of an event, leading to different experiences and interpretations.

Past experiences and conditioning. Our past experiences and conditioning significantly influence how we perceive and interpret present events. Previous encounters, learned behaviors, and emotional associations can create biases or predispositions that color our perception. For example, someone who has had negative experiences with dogs may perceive a dog encounter as threatening, while another person with positive experiences may perceive it as enjoyable. Our past shapes our present experiences, and these differences accumulate over time.

Individual beliefs and worldviews. Our beliefs and worldviews act as powerful filters through which we interpret reality. Our beliefs about ourselves, others, and the world shape our expectations, judgments, and reactions. These beliefs can be influenced by factors such as culture, religion, upbringing, education, and personal values. Consequently, two people with different belief systems can perceive and interpret the same event in contrasting ways, based on their underlying assumptions and perspectives.

Attention and focus. Our attention determines what we focus on and how we use our mental resources. Two people may have different priorities, interests, or concerns, leading them to attend to different aspects of a situation. For example, in a crowded room, one person may focus on the interactions between people, while another may be more attuned to the room's aesthetics or the ambient sounds. This selective attention can result in distinct experiences, even when one is observing the same event.

Emotional state and well-being. Our emotional state can heavily influence our experiences and interpretations. When we are in a positive emotional state, we may be more inclined to notice positive aspects of a situation, whereas negative emotions can narrow our focus and lead us to perceive events more negatively. Additionally, two people with different levels of overall well-being and mental health may have different cognitive biases and interpret events through the lens of their emotional states.

While two people may observe the same external event, their internal processes and subjective filters shape how they interpret and respond to it. Recognizing these differences can foster empathy, understanding, and appreciation for the unique perspectives that each person brings to the world.

The Stick Person

The answer to this question lies in the Stick Person. The Stick Person is a graphic that was created by Dr. Thurman Fleet, a chiropractor and metaphysical teacher, which helps us to understand the relationship between the conscious mind, the subconscious mind, and the body.

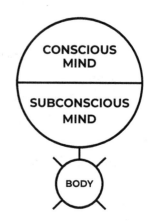

The Conscious Mind

At the top, you'll see the conscious mind. This is our intellect, thoughts, emotions, decisions, and free will. It's what we normally think of as our mind and consists of the thoughts we hear in our heads as we go about our day. In the case of Chris in our example above, it's where he makes the decision to be a sculptor despite his dad's objections.

Here's how it works. We walk into a room full of people, and we experience sensory input. We hear voices and see people and tables and chairs. We may feel hot or cold and smell food or someone's perfume. We could taste the gum we are chewing and feel the weight of our jacket. Those senses trigger conscious thoughts and feelings: "I'm feeling really nervous right now. What if I don't fit in? Where is my friend sitting? Why does this room smell like garlic?"

When we allow our senses to direct our thoughts, we are experiencing "what is." We are observing the current moment with no thought to how we might influence it.

The intellect is also part of the conscious mind. The imagination or will can direct our thoughts to something that isn't yet in our present reality: "If I can find my friend and sit with them, this will be a fun evening." This isn't a direct observation, but rather a thought that is guided by your intellect and will. These thoughts are influenced by your past experiences as well. If you think, "The last time I was at an event like this, I was completely bored and hated it," you're telling your subconscious mind something different than if you think, "This could be fun!"

The conscious mind is the part of you that accepts or rejects ideas. The thoughts that you consciously choose will eventually determine your life because they will be imprinted onto your subconscious mind. This is true for thoughts that come from outside (other people) and those that from inside (your own memories and ideas).

> No person or event can force you
> to think thoughts you don't want.

Accept a thought with your conscious mind will direct it to the subconscious mind without question. This is very important for several reasons. It allows us to understand how "thoughts become things." You choose an idea, your conscious mind accepts it, and the subconscious mind receives it. Conscious accepting and rejecting of thoughts allow us to change what shows up in our lives.

In our example above, Chris is continually being exposed to messaging that he isn't good enough—from his dad, who wants him to have a stable career, to his mentor, who is telling him to change his artistic style. Whether he realizes it or not, Chris is accepting what they tell him. This then translates into rejection after rejection by art galleries.

The key is for Chris to challenge the ideas that he is accepting as truth and reject the ones that don't serve what he wants in his life. Remember the exercise in the last chapter where we explored the differences between a memory and a movie? The things Chris is told by his dad and John are nothing more than thoughts in his head. He can consciously choose to accept or reject them.

The Subconscious Mind

In the graphic above, the next thing we see is the subconscious mind. This is the invisible "life force" that runs through your body. It operates as a paradigm for every aspect of your life. These are the unquestioned ideas and ways you see your world. These paradigms stay until they are consciously changed.

If your conscious mind has accepted the idea that people with money are selfish and greedy and use other people for their personal gain, your subconscious mind isn't going to question that. It becomes a template for how you behave. Even if the idea is untrue, the subconscious mind cannot reject it. The subconscious mind will accept every thought or word the conscious mind chooses to accept.

This is wonderful news for us! It means that the subconscious mind knows no limits other than the ones we put into it. If we change that, we can change our lives. This is how the ideas in this book work: you are learning to consciously choose the thoughts that you are putting into your subconscious mind, and your subconscious mind has no choice to accept them, *even if they're not currently true!* We must shift our thinking from observing "what is" to thinking about the potential of "what can be."

The Body

The final part of the graphic is the body. Most of us identify more with our bodies than with our minds. But we are so much more than our physical bodies! The body simply performs the actions that are prescribed by the mind. It's an instrument of the mind.

Thoughts lead to *feelings*, which lead to *actions*, which create *results*.

In our scenario above, Chris is being told by his dad and his mentor, John, that he's not good enough to be a sculptor (thoughts). This leads him to feel insecure about his talent (feelings), so he tries to adapt his style to be more like John's (actions). This creates artwork that isn't very good (results) because it's not Chris's style, it's John's.

Instead, Chris can use the power of his conscious mind to reject his dad's and John's ideas: "They're wrong. My work is good enough for me to make it as a sculptor" (thoughts). This leads him to raise his self-esteem (feelings), and he embraces his natural style of sculpting. He leaves his apprenticeship with John and finds galleries that display art that's more like his own style (actions). He is thrilled to find that his work is easily accepted in those galleries, and he starts selling his pieces (results).

Quiz: What's in My Subconscious?

Circle the statements that apply to you. Do this quickly without thinking too much about your response. Circle the ones that might apply even if you're not sure.

1. I find it hard to ask for what I am worth financially.
2. I have negative feelings about or am envious of wealthy people.
3. Someone else outside of me is responsible for my financial situation.
4. I am proud of my ability to get the best price on things.
5. I have a family history of debt or financial problems.
6. I keep trying to make more money but never seem to be able to break through.
7. I am good at managing money, but there's never enough to go around.
8. It takes hard work and many hours to become wealthy.
9. I feel I'm never going to be able to achieve my financial goals.

10. No matter how much I achieve, I'm always looking for the next goal.
11. I love money and what it can do for my life.
12. I believe I can change my financial future.
13. I am willing to take consistent action to achieve my goals.
14. I am passionate about my work.
15. There are some wealthy people that I consider to be role models or mentors.
16. I have no problem asking to be paid what I am worth.
17. Most of the time, I feel grateful for the life I am living.
18. Every day I am getting better than I was the day before.
19. I am tenacious and disciplined in achieving the goals I want to achieve.
20. No one can hold me back from my dreams.

Scoring. If you circled more of questions 1–10, your subconscious mind has received some negative programming that is likely affecting your financial abundance. If you circled more questions from 11 to 20, you are likely already experiencing wealth and are ready to take it to the next level.

Mike's Story

A few years back, I was coaching an energy industry executive that we'll call Mike. From the outside, he seemed to have everything a person could want. He lived in a high-end condo with the finest amenities, had two sports cars in the garage and another luxury car as his daily driver, and took his family on expensive vacations every year. But Mike felt he was running on a treadmill that kept speeding up. He was working sixty-hour weeks just to keep up with his work and afford his lifestyle. He started having health problems—largely because he wasn't eating well and never used the expensive exercise equipment in his home or office.

"Arash," he said, "this is no way to live. Yes, I have financial wealth. But I am not free. I'm chained to my job like a workhorse."

Through our coaching, Mike started to grasp some of the core ideas in this book. The four pillars of wealth aren't just about getting more money and belongings. Like Mike, you can have all of those things and still be miserable. This book is about building a life of freedom, where you have the things you want *and* a life that brings you peace and pleasure.

In our coaching sessions, Mike discovered the power of his conscious mind to reprogram his subconscious mind, leading to a transformation in his beliefs about money. He recognized that certain limiting beliefs were holding him back from experiencing true abundance and enjoying life to the fullest. With determination and guidance, he embarked on a journey of reshaping his mindset and adopting empowering beliefs that aligned with his desired reality.

One belief that Mike had to address was the notion that successful people must own multiple sports cars. This belief was likely rooted in societal expectations or comparisons to others' material possessions. Through introspection and coaching exercises, Mike realized that true success and fulfillment were not solely defined by material possessions. He learned to redefine success based on his own values, aspirations, and what brought him genuine joy and contentment. By releasing the attachment to external symbols of success, Mike found freedom to pursue a more balanced and fulfilling life.

Mike also had to confront the limiting belief that he had to work harder than most people to achieve financial abundance. This belief, while commonly ingrained in society, can create a mindset of constant striving and burnout. Through coaching discussions and mindset exercises, Mike began to shift his perspective. He understood that wealth creation was not solely dependent on working harder but also on working smarter, leveraging his strengths, and embracing opportunities. He realized the importance of aligning his actions with his goals, making strategic choices, and optimizing his efforts for maximum effectiveness and efficiency.

By consciously reprogramming his subconscious mind with new beliefs, Mike experienced a significant shift in his approach to money and life. He understood that abundance and success were not limited resources reserved for a select few but were available to anyone who cultivated the right mindset and took inspired action. Mike learned to slow down, enjoy the journey, and appreciate the present moment while pursuing his financial goals. He embraced the idea that true wealth encompasses not only financial prosperity but also overall well-being, fulfilling relationships, personal growth, and a sense of purpose.

Through consistent practice and reinforcement, Mike integrated these empowering beliefs into his daily life. He surrounded himself with positive influences, engaged in gratitude practices, visualizations, and affirmations to reinforce his new mindset. Over time, Mike experienced a profound transformation in his relationship with money. He found a greater sense of peace, fulfillment, and abundance, not only in his financial circumstances but also in his overall quality of life.

Mike's journey highlights the immense power of the conscious mind to reshape our beliefs and ultimately our reality. By challenging and replacing limiting beliefs with empowering ones, we can create a positive and abundant mindset that paves the way for personal growth, success, and a more fulfilling life.

In the next chapter, we'll go into the first of the four pillars: Image.

3

Image

Stacy Farmer was so thrilled she almost couldn't believe it. She just sat there, looking at her income tax form: "This was the year I finally broke into a six-figure income." Stacy had been trying her whole life to break through, but no matter what she did, it never seemed to work.

Eager to share the news, she called her mentor. "I did it! I earned $105,000 last year!" When her mentor asked what she thought made the difference, Stacy exclaimed, "I don't know! It just finally happened."

Her mentor knew better. For the past couple of years, Stacy had been meeting with him to change her mindset about wealth. One comment in particular stood out: "Until I saw myself as the kind of person who could actually earn that kind of money, I believed it was out of reach. It just seemed like a dream for sometime in the future. But when I realized that I could actually do it, something fundamental shifted. And, I'm not stopping here!"

Every person on the planet who is over the age of, say, five has a self-image. At first, our self-image is crafted by the adults around us. If we were raised in a loving environment, feeling wanted, and with plenty of resources to go around, we grew up to believe that we were worthy of good things. But if we were raised in an environment that was not ideal, our self-image might not have been as strong.

As we saw in the previous chapter, the conscious mind is the place where we accept or reject thoughts. Furthermore, the subconscious mind accepts without question the thoughts that it receives from the conscious mind. But as children, we don't have the critical thinking skills to challenge the thoughts that we were given. This is true whether the ideas are about ourselves or the world around us. Children believe what they are told. Even more importantly, children believe what they see. If a child's parents struggle financially, have a poverty mindset, speak and act negatively around those who have financial success, the child will absorb those ideas, and they will become embedded in the subconscious. This creates a program that becomes the "operating system" for the child's mind. That program will influence the child's actions. "I'll never be able to go to college," he or she might say. "No one in my family has gone to college, and we could never afford it." As a result, the child doesn't work hard in school or explore scholarship opportunities. It's not even on his or her radar that higher education is possible.

You Can Never Outperform Your self-image

Your self-image is made up of how you see yourself, how you observe your own actions, whether you make changes when needed, and whether or not you expand yourself. It reflects how you perceive yourself, how you interpret your own actions and behaviors, and whether you are open to growth and personal development. It plays a crucial role in shaping your beliefs, attitudes, and behaviors, ultimately influencing your outcomes.

Creating a significant self-image involves cultivating a positive and empowering perception of yourself that aligns with your true potential and aspirations. It's about recognizing your inherent worth, embracing your strengths, and acknowledging the value you bring to the world.

Self-image isn't a fixed concept. It evolves and expands over time as you gain new experiences, learn from challenges, and actively work on personal growth. You can change it. Have you created a significant image of yourself? If not, you need an update.

Upgrade Your Programming

Self-image psychology has been around for more than fifty years. Frankly, it's probably been around a lot longer than that, but people didn't talk or write about it as much. It was more of a secret mindset that wealthy people knew and kept to themselves.

No one can give you a positive self-image. Once you've reached the age where you can think independently from the adults around you, you are responsible for your opinion of yourself. I can't give you a positive self-image, nor can this book do it for you—you have to do it for yourself. We'll get more into how you do that in a later chapter of this book.

The results you see in your life now reflect your self-image. Your income, your bank account, the amount of debt you have, your health, and the quality of your relationships are all mirrors of how you see yourself. In order to raise the level of your life, you have to raise your self-image. It is the foundation of your internal program.

> You can never outperform your self-image,
> but you can change it.

Henry's Story

Sarah is a human resources manager at a medium-sized marketing firm. She's been married to her husband, Henry, for twenty years and in that time has become the breadwinner for their family. They've got two kids, Xander and Abby, and Xander has just gone off to college. Throughout their marriage, Henry has tried to start several businesses, each one failing for one reason or another. At first, this caused tension in the marriage: Sarah didn't feel it was fair that she worked so hard to earn money for the family while her husband kept losing money in his failed startups.

It was hard on Henry as well. He'd been programmed by his family to believe that the man was the one who supported his wife and children. Moreover, the small town where he lived still looked down upon stay-at-home dads. So Henry was feeling like a failure, who couldn't do anything right.

Sarah came upon my work through a training program offered by her company, and she immediately told Henry about it. He began to realize that his businesses had failed because he never identified as a business owner. He'd seen himself as a "guy with creative ideas." When he discovered the tools that allowed him to shift his self-image to that of a successful business owner, things began to take off. He met a team of people who were experts in different areas of business, and they began to create a solid foundation for a company. Within five years, the business was turning a profit, and Henry saw the results he'd always wanted. It all happened after he brought his self-image into harmony with what he really wanted.

If your self-image is out of harmony with what you want, you'll never achieve it. Your job is to identify what you want and bring your self-image into harmony with your goals. Otherwise, it can create internal conflicts and limit your ability to manifest your desired outcomes. Therefore it becomes essential to identify what you truly want and work towards aligning your self-image with those aspirations.

Aligning Goals with Self-Image

Here are some key points to consider when aligning your self-image with your goals.

Clarify your desires. Clearly define what you want to achieve or experience in different areas of your life. This could include career goals, relationships, health, personal growth, or any other aspect that matters to you. Be specific and detailed in your descriptions. We have a worksheet later in the book that can help you do that.

Assess your current self-image. Reflect on how you currently perceive yourself and whether it aligns with the person who would naturally achieve your desired goals. Identify any beliefs, habits, or thought patterns that may be incongruent with your aspirations. This self-assessment helps you identify areas you need to adjust.

Challenge limiting beliefs. Examine any limiting beliefs or self-doubts that may be holding you back. These are often subconscious thoughts that undermine your confidence and prevent you from fully embracing your potential. Replace them with empowering beliefs that support your goals and affirm your ability to achieve them.

Visualization and affirmations. Utilize visualization and affirmations as powerful tools to align your self-image with your goals. Regularly visualize yourself as already in possession of your desired outcomes, engaging in the necessary actions, and experiencing the associated emotions. Reinforce these visualizations with positive affirmations that affirm your capabilities and reinforce your belief in achieving your goals.

Take aligned action. Align your actions with your desired self-image and goals. Consistently take steps that are congruent with the person you want to become and the outcomes you wish to manifest. This includes adopting new habits, acquiring relevant skills and knowledge, seeking opportunities, and embracing growth-oriented experiences.

Embrace growth and adaptation. Recognize that aligning your self-image with your goals is a journey of growth and adaptation. Be open to learning, adjusting your approach, and overcoming challenges along the way. Embrace the process of personal evolution as you strive to bring your self-image into harmony with your aspirations.

Your Biggest Insecurities Are Your Biggest Opportunities

Most of us have areas where we are insecure. I'm here to tell you that you shouldn't be afraid of your insecurities. They aren't obstacles on your path to success. They are the gifts of growth.

Let's do a little exercise. On a sheet of paper, I want you to write out your five biggest insecurities about yourself. It could look something like this:

1. I don't have a formal education.
2. I'm bad at managing money.
3. I'm too young (or old) to achieve my goals.
4. I'm stuck in a job I hate.
5. I'm not brave enough to take risks.

Now write out how each of these insecurities provides gifts of growth. How can you use these insecurities to grow? Your list might look like this:

1. I can go back to school online or on weekends.
2. I can learn how to manage money.
3. I can meet other people my age who have achieved their goals and learn from them.
4. I can look for a different job and learn what I need to know to get hired.
5. I can practice taking small risks and learn to become braver.

> The best way to raise your self-image is through action.

Here's the most important action you can take right now: **Make a definite, irrevocable committed decision to do whatever it takes, not what's convenient.** Accept extreme ownership of your life. What you do right now will dictate future results. Don't start later, start now. Every day is day one.

You Are Your Only Problem and Your Only Solution

That may sound harsh, but it's true. Everything that has happened to you in your past now exists only in your mind. If they are still problems and are holding you back, then *you* are your problem.

But you are also the only solution you'll ever have. You are the only one who can change your self-image. Sprint toward your insecurities. They are not the problem. Your problem is your attitude toward your insecurities.

Self-image is the most important picture you have of yourself. Create a more significant and positive opinion of yourself, and watch your life change with it. Big things are ahead for you. Everything has led you up to this point. Another person is inside you, dying to get out. Your soul wants you to express yourself.

The Power of Grace

Often when things don't go as planned, we beat ourselves up, generating a loop of negative self-talk that is imprinted into the subconscious mind: "I am so stupid. How could I have let that happen? They are right about me. I am beyond hope and can never achieve my goals."

Instead, how about showing yourself a little bit of grace? Even when you made the biggest mistakes—didn't take actions, didn't follow through on things—cut yourself some slack and give yourself grace.

This doesn't mean making excuses for failure. Instead, take responsibility for what happened, and move on: "Look, it happened, and I can't change the past. But I'm not going to beat myself up about it. I'll just do better going forward."

> Giving ourselves grace raises our self-image.

It Worked for Me

I know this to be true because it worked for me. I created the biggest quantum leap when I changed my image.

I had been doing this work forever, and it didn't seem to be having any effect. Despite investing considerable time and effort into personal growth and development, I found myself repeating the same patterns and obtaining the same unsatisfactory results. I reached a pivotal moment in my journey where I realized that in order to create a significant change in my life, I needed to shift my self-image.

At this point, someone imparted a profound insight to me: "Arash, you are stuck gathering information, not taking action on what you learned."

This person's words struck a chord within me. I had become too focused on accumulating information without acting decisively on what I had learned. I realized that it was not enough to passively absorb information or seek guidance from mentors. Instead, I needed to become an active participant in my own transformation by aligning my thoughts, beliefs, and actions with the person I aspired to be—the one who already possessed the outcomes I sought. This process required a mindful and deliberate refusal to accept anything that contradicted my desired self-image. Through changing my self-image and aligning my thoughts and actions accordingly, I experienced a quantum leap in my life.

If we want to change our self-image, we have to engage our mind and our emotions. It begins with the power of thought—a conscious decision to reject anything that contradicts or hinders the realization of our desired self-image. We must develop an unwavering resolve, uttering a resolute *no* to any thoughts, beliefs, or behaviors that do not align with our true aspirations.

This process goes beyond mere wishful thinking or positive affirmations: it requires deep introspection and an understanding of the values, qualities, and attributes of our desired self-image. Consistent mental discipline and vigilance are required to identify and replace any thoughts or beliefs that undermine our progress. By consciously choosing thoughts that support and reinforce our desired self-image, we lay the foundation for transformational action.

Embracing this mindset shift empowers us to bridge the gap between where we are and where we want to be. It activates our potential, propelling us towards a life that reflects our true aspirations and desires. By aligning our thoughts, words, and actions with our desired self-image, we embody the qualities that are necessary to manifest the outcomes we seek.

Although mentorship and guidance are invaluable resources, they alone cannot guarantee results. The true catalyst for change lies in our own commitment to take bold and decisive action. Unwavering determination to act consistently and persistently in harmony with our envisioned self will propel us forward on our transformative journey.

By harnessing the power of our minds and taking decisive action, we pave the way for profound personal transformation and the realization of our most cherished aspirations.

Just because you invest in mentorship doesn't mean you'll automatically get the results. You have to *do* something. You have to act in harmony with the person you want to be and the person who has what you want.

To change your self-image, you have to use your mind. You have to think. You have to think and say a hard *no* to anything that isn't in harmony with what you want.

Opening the Gates

At one point, my wife and I were considering a house to purchase. We had achieved a certain level of financial success, and the house we were about to see was well within our means. As we arrived at the property, I couldn't help noticing the grandeur of the huge gate that greeted us. It stood as a symbol of luxury and success, yet it also triggered a profound internal dialogue.

As I walked through that gate, a voice echoed in my mind, asking, "Who do you think you are, Arash?" In that instant, a wave of realization washed over me, revealing the work that I still needed to do on my self-image. It became clear that I was seeking validation from external sources rather than relying on my own inner strength and belief in myself.

This poignant moment served as a catalyst for introspection. I recognized that my self-image was not fully aligned with my true aspirations and desires. It was a humbling yet empowering realization that led me to question the ideas and beliefs that had influenced my self-perception.

By confronting this discrepancy, I embarked on a transformative journey of self-discovery and self-mastery. I resolved to reject any ideas or thoughts that were out of harmony with the person I truly wanted to become. I understood that allowing external circumstances or the opinions of others to define me would only hinder my progress and fulfillment.

With renewed determination, I committed myself to elevating my self-image and aligning it with my deepest aspirations. I immersed myself in personal development practices, fostering self-acceptance, self-love, and an unwavering belief in my own worth. This process demanded introspection, reflection, and a willingness to challenge long-held beliefs that no longer served my highest potential.

As time went on, I began to witness the profound effects of this transformation. We eventually found ourselves purchasing a different house—one that exceeded our initial expectations. This new achievement was a testament to the power of aligning my self-image with my true desires and rejecting any limiting beliefs or doubts. It all happened because a voice in my head told me that my image wasn't in harmony with what I really wanted.

This experience served as a profound lesson: we must be the architects of our own self-image, carefully crafting it to reflect the person we aspire to be. Through this intentional alignment of thoughts, beliefs, and desires, we can create the life we truly want.

It is crucial not to allow external results or setbacks to dictate our behavior or undermine our belief in ourselves. Instead, we must remain steadfast in our commitment to our authentic self and reject any ideas that do not align with our true essence. By doing so, we reclaim our power to shape our own destiny and manifest the life we envision.

I encourage you to embark on a similar journey of self-discovery and self-mastery. Embrace the process of aligning your self-image with your deepest aspirations, and consciously choose thoughts, beliefs, and actions that are in harmony with the person you want to become. Remember, your results do not define you; it is your unwavering belief in yourself and your ability to reject limiting ideas that will ultimately shape your path to success and fulfillment.

Reject ideas that are out of harmony with who you want to be. You can't let your results dictate your behavior.

If It Worked for One Person, It Can Work for You

One of the most powerful thoughts that you can accept in your conscious mind is that if one person has achieved something, so can you. As Stacy in our opening story experienced, once you shift your image to that of someone who can achieve what you want, then—and only then—can you get it.

When I work with clients, one of the fundamental areas we focus on is their self-image. I firmly believe that establishing a strong and empowering self-image serves as the foundation for personal growth and transformation. Through this process, you can tap into the extraordinary potential that resides within you—a version of yourself that is powerful beyond measure.

Together, my client and I embark on a journey of self-exploration and self-awareness, peeling back the layers that have shaped their current self-image. We delve deeply into the beliefs, experiences, and conditioning that have influenced how they perceive themselves and their capabilities. By shining a light on these factors, we gain valuable insights into the patterns and limitations that may be holding them back.

The process begins with creating a safe and supportive space for clients to reflect on their self-perception. Through open and honest dialogue, we explore the thoughts, emotions, and behaviors that are rooted in their current self-image. This introspection allows them to gain clarity on the aspects of their self-image that no longer serve their highest potential.

As their coach and guide, I encourage them to recognize that they are not confined to their current self-image. We work together to expand their understanding and help them see the limitless possibilities that exist within them. It is essential for them to comprehend that they possess a reservoir of untapped power and potential, just waiting to be unleashed.

Through a series of empowering exercises and practices (which I share in a later chapter of this book), we start reshaping their self-image. We challenge any self-limiting beliefs and replace them with empowering thoughts and affirmations that align with their true desires. Visualization techniques and guided meditations allow them to vividly imagine and embody the powerful version of themselves they aspire to be.

It is a gradual process, and requires patience, dedication, and self-compassion. Yet as we progress, I witness a beautiful transformation. Clients begin to shed the limitations that once held them back and embrace a more expansive self-image. They become more aware of their unique strengths, talents, and qualities. With each breakthrough, their confidence grows, and they step into their innate power and authenticity.

Working on self-image is not about creating an artificial or inflated sense of self. Instead, it is about unlocking clients' true potential and embracing the best version of themselves. It is about recognizing their inherent worth and realizing that they are capable of achieving remarkable things.

As their coach, I celebrate every milestone and encourage clients to continue embracing their newfound self-image. We integrate this empowering self-perception into their daily lives, ensuring that it becomes a natural and authentic part of who they are. With time and practice, their powerful self-image becomes their default mode of thinking, influencing their actions, decisions, and ultimately their outcomes.

Witnessing clients embrace their powerful self-image and witnessing its positive impact on their lives is incredibly fulfilling. They step into their personal and professional endeavors with newfound courage, resilience, and determination. Challenges and setbacks no longer deter them, as they understand that their true power lies within their self-perception and unwavering belief in themselves.

Working on self-image is a transformative process that allows clients to tap into a version of themselves that is powerful beyond measure. By shedding self-limiting beliefs, embracing their innate worth, and aligning their thoughts and actions with their desired self-image, they unlock their true potential. Through this work, clients embark on a journey of self-discovery, empowerment, and personal growth, ultimately creating a life that reflects their most powerful and authentic self.

> Your spiritual DNA doesn't need any modification. It is perfect the way it is.
> You can tap into the power that creates worlds.
> As we become aware of this, you're operating from your higher self.

Where do you want to strengthen your image? Choose the areas where you want to grow, and strengthen your image in that area. We'll have some more specific exercises and actions in a later chapter of this book. But for now, understand that your self-image impacts every aspect of your life.

In the next chapter, we'll start to explore your personal Standard and how it affects your life.

> Today's self-image creates future results.

4

Standard

As the flight attendant's voice came over the speaker, saying, "We are beginning our final descent into Charles de Gaulle airport," Caryn was terrified. She'd just started her first job after getting her MBA and was part of a team getting ready to make an important presentation to a Paris-based client. No one else on the team was available to travel, so she had to make the trip on her own. Typically, this kind of project was reserved for a more senior consultant—one who'd been at the company at least five years. Caryn had never been to Europe and had never traveled alone. This was a make-or-break moment for her, and she knew that if she blew this presentation, it would change the trajectory of her entire career.

"I have to make this work," she thought as the wheels of the plane touched down in France. "I've just got to feel the fear and do it anyway."

It worked. Not only was the presentation a huge success, but Caryn was promoted faster than anyone ever had been in her firm. Her attitude was, "No matter what someone asks you to do (unless it's illegal or unethical, of course), say yes and figure out how to do it."

Your Standard Is Your DNA to Success

Your personal Standard serves as a benchmark for the quality of life you are willing to accept and experience. It's the minimum level of excellence, fulfillment, and achievement that you demand from yourself and from the circumstances and opportunities that come your way. It reflects your self-image, your values, and your aspirations.

Your personal Standard is the bare minimum that you'll accept in your life. To raise the quality of your life, you have to raise your Standard. Once you do, your life changes forever, because you'll do whatever it takes not to fall below your new, raised Standard. You can never go back, unless you lower your Standard.

When you raise your Standard, you are telling the universe in no uncertain terms, "I am no longer willing to accept anything less than what I truly want." It is a powerful declaration that you deserve more, that you are capable of more, and that you are committed to creating a life that aligns with your highest vision.

By raising your Standard, you initiate a profound shift in your mindset and behavior. You no longer settle for mediocrity, complacency, or stagnation. Instead, you embrace a mindset of growth, excellence, and continuous improvement. You become determined to go beyond your comfort zone, stretch your limits, and consistently strive for greater success and fulfillment. That determination will show up as committed action that leads you to your goal.

Once you raise your Standard, your life undergoes a remarkable transformation. You start to attract new opportunities, relationships, and experiences that are in alignment with your elevated expectations. Your focus shifts towards excellence, and you become more proactive, resourceful, and resilient in pursuing your goals. Challenges and setbacks no longer deter you: they become opportunities for growth and learning.

When you establish a new, raised Standard, you develop a powerful commitment and resolve to maintain it. You understand that settling for anything less would compromise your self-respect and hinder your progress. You adopt a relentless attitude of doing whatever it takes to uphold your elevated Standard, even in the face of obstacles or temptations to regress.

The decision to raise your Standard is a pivotal moment that shifts your internal program forever. You can never go back to the way things were. Instead, you develop new habits, routines, and rituals that support your growth and success. You surround yourself with people who share similar values and aspirations, and you create a supportive network that reinforces your commitment to excellence.

Once you have raised your Standard, going back to a lower level of expectation or achievement becomes increasingly difficult. The transformation you experience, the progress you make, and the rewards you reap reinforce the belief that you are capable of more. The prospect of reverting to a lesser Standard becomes unappealing and incongruent with your newfound sense of self and potential.

That being said, it is crucial to remain vigilant about the thoughts we entertain and the choices we make on a daily basis. You can't let your guard down and start accepting the things you used to accept. You have to stay aware of your new Standard and continue to reject anything that doesn't meet it.

Maintaining a high Standard requires an ongoing commitment to self-awareness, self-discipline, and self-compassion. Life has a way of presenting us with temptations, setbacks, and unexpected circumstances, which may challenge our resolve to uphold our raised Standard. But during these moments of testing, our true character and unwavering determination come to the forefront.

> When we are tested, our true character and unwavering determination come to the forefront.

Sustaining an elevated Standard demands continuous examination of our thoughts, beliefs, and behaviors. We must regularly assess whether they align with the values and principles we hold dear. This self-reflection allows us to identify any potential deviations or compromises that could lower our Standard. By cultivating self-awareness, we remain attuned to our inner dialogue and the influences that shape our mindset.

Like self-awareness, self-discipline plays a crucial role in upholding our Standard. It requires a resolute commitment to making choices and acting in alignment with our highest aspirations. Even when faced with alluring shortcuts or temporary gratifications, we must exercise self-discipline and choose the path that is consistent with our raised Standard. This may involve making sacrifices, delaying gratification, or embracing discomfort in pursuit of long-term fulfillment and growth.

While upholding a high Standard is essential, it is equally important to treat ourselves with self-compassion along the way. We are human beings, and it is natural to encounter moments of weakness or lapses in judgment. However, these moments give us the opportunity to learn, grow, and reaffirm our commitment to our raised Standard. Instead of berating ourselves for perceived shortcomings, we can view these instances as valuable lessons that contribute to our personal development. Through self-compassion, we cultivate a nurturing environment that supports our ongoing journey towards excellence.

Upholding a high Standard is not always easy. Life's challenges and unexpected circumstances can test our resolve and present us with difficult choices. However, these moments of adversity reveal our true character and determination. In these moments, our commitment to our raised Standard shines through, allowing us to navigate challenges with integrity and unwavering dedication.

Maintaining a high Standard requires continuous vigilance and mindfulness. It involves an ongoing commitment to self-awareness, self-discipline, and self-compassion. While life may present us with temptations, setbacks, and challenging circumstances, our true character is demonstrated by our ability to uphold our Standard even in the face of adversity. By remaining steadfast in our commitment to excellence, we cultivate a life guided by integrity, authenticity, and personal fulfillment.

Your personal Standard serves as the foundation for your quality of life. By raising your Standard, you open yourself up to a world of new possibilities, growth, and fulfillment. It becomes a catalyst for lasting change and empowers you to transcend previous limitations. Your elevated Standard becomes a guiding principle that fuels your actions, shapes your mindset, and propels you towards a life of greater success, happiness, and fulfillment.

Aymee's Story

Aymee came to me for mindset coaching because she felt her life had gotten out of control. Her husband, an airport security guard, worked long hours, and she was left home alone to raise her three children. She'd joined a network marketing company and wanted to make some income selling makeup and skin care products but wasn't having much success.

She told me a story about the moment she realized she needed to raise her Standard. Her baby had an ear infection, and she'd been up almost all night comforting the crying infant. When the baby finally fell asleep, Aymee and her twelve-year-old daughter left the father to watch the baby and went to the market for a few items. Aymee hadn't put any thought into what she was wearing or how she looked; she was more concerned about getting to and from the market before the baby woke up. As she and her daughter were in the produce section, Aymee saw a woman from her network marketing team. She suddenly realized that she was wearing flannel pajama pants and a T-shirt that had seen better days. Ducking behind a crate of potatoes, Aymee said to her daughter, "Quick. Get down here before she sees us." Instead, Aymee's daughter looked at her and said, "Mom, maybe if you don't want people seeing you in your pajamas, don't wear your pajamas out of the house."

That was a wake-up call for Aymee. She was trying to promote beauty products, but her personal appearance wasn't reflecting her brand. For Aymee, raising her Standard meant making sure that she looked and acted the part of a successful beauty brand ambassador every time she left the house.

When it comes to setting your personal Standard, it's essential to ask yourself how you truly want to live. Reflect on the contribution you want to make in this world. Consider the impact you aspire to have on others and the legacy you want to leave behind.

In addition to making a meaningful contribution, think about how you want to spend your days. Envision the activities, pursuits, and relationships that bring you joy and fulfillment. Consider how you can align your daily life with your passions and interests, creating a sense of purpose and satisfaction.

It's also crucial to examine your current self-perception and envision the person you want to become. Fall in love with your future self and the possibilities that lie ahead. Embrace personal growth and development as an ongoing journey, continuously evolving into the best version of yourself. Define the values and principles that will guide your actions and decisions, and then set your Standard based on them.

One empowering realization is that you have the ability to create your own Standard of living. While money is often associated with wealth, true wealth lies in the person you become. Focus on cultivating qualities such as integrity, resilience, kindness, and compassion. Strive to make a positive impact on others and contribute to the well-being of society as a whole.

Your Future Starts as a Want for Something Different

Goals play a pivotal role in shaping your personal Standard. They provide a vision of your desired future and serve as a roadmap for your journey. But the future life you're creating doesn't start as a goal. It starts as a *want for a difference*. "I want to become financially free" isn't enough, but it's a crucial first start.

It's important to differentiate between a mere want and a goal. A want is simply a desire or preference, while a goal involves a deeper level of commitment and intention. To transform a want into a goal, you must become emotionally invested in it. Through this emotional involvement, you create a passion for achieving the goal. From this place of emotional engagement, you can truly start leading yourself.

Set stretch goals, which challenge you to grow and expand beyond your comfort zone. These goals should inspire and excite you, igniting a sense of passion and purpose.

Achieving your goals requires making conscious decisions along the way. Consider the decisions you will need to make in order to align your actions with your aspirations. Evaluate the potential trade-offs and sacrifices you may need to make in pursuit of your goals. Embrace the responsibility that comes with your decisions and be willing to make choices that support your personal Standard.

Success Is Getting 1 Percent Better Every Day

To become successful, focus on improving 1 percent every day. Explore various perspectives on success, including those of notable inspirational figures like Earl Nightingale and Napoleon Hill.

Success is the progression realization of a worthy goal or ideal.
—EARL NIGHTINGALE

Success is the attainment of your Definite Chief Aim
without violating the rights of others.
—NAPOLEON HILL

Success is doing what you want, when you want, where you want, with whom you want as much as you want. That's a powerful purpose.
—ANTHONY ROBBINS

What's your definition of success?

Ultimately, it's important to develop your own definition of success, one that resonates with your values and aspirations. Consider success as an ongoing journey of self-improvement and growth, with the aim of consistently beating your personal best.

Strive to become 1 percent better every day, embracing incremental progress and continuous improvement.

Setting your personal Standard is a process of self-reflection, goal-setting, and conscious decision-making. Consider the contribution you want to make, how you want to spend your days, and the person you aspire to become. Understand that true wealth lies in personal growth and character development. Set stretch goals that challenge you to grow and define success on your own terms. Embrace the journey of becoming the best version of yourself and continuously striving for improvement.

Everyone has a Standard. You want to consciously create a Standard that's in harmony with how you want to live.

I firmly believe that our personal Standard is the DNA of success. It is intricately correlated with our self-image and plays a pivotal role in shaping our lives. Our Standard sets the bar for what we are willing to accept, and it becomes a powerful guiding force in our pursuit of growth and achievement. It is the unwavering declaration that states, "I am not accepting anything under this level."

To consciously create your Standard, you must possess the discipline to say no to anything or anyone who tempts you to regress into your old ways. It requires strength and resolve to reject anything that falls below the level you have set for yourself. This applies to all aspects of your life: relationships, career, health, or personal development.

Setting a Standard for every area of your life is crucial. It provides clarity and direction, and it enables you to make conscious choices that align with your highest aspirations. As you define your standards, remember that they are not static but rather dynamic and ever-evolving. The Standard you set today should continually rise as you grow and expand your horizons.

These standards become your nonnegotiables, the guiding principles by which you navigate your life. They are the values and expectations that you hold true to, even in the face of challenges and temptations. By upholding these nonnegotiables, you build integrity and self-respect. You demonstrate to yourself and others that you are committed to living a life of excellence.

Standard Always Wins

Change starts with setting a higher Standard. Even if you make no other changes in your life, raising your Standard alone can have a profound impact. By refusing to settle for mediocrity, you invite greatness into your life. You open doors to new opportunities, forge deeper connections, and unlock your true potential.

Creating your Standard requires self-awareness and reflection. Take the time to evaluate what truly matters to you and what you aspire to achieve. Identify the areas of your life where you have been settling for less than you deserve. Make a conscious decision to raise your standards in those areas, and commit to upholding them unwaveringly.

Remember that creating your Standard is a journey, not a destination. It is an ongoing process of growth and refinement. Embrace the challenges and setbacks along the way as opportunities for learning and growth. Celebrate your progress and acknowledge the positive changes that arise from consciously raising your Standard.

Consciously creating your Standard is a powerful catalyst for personal transformation. It sets the foundation for success and becomes the guiding force in your pursuit of a fulfilling life. Embrace the power of your Standard, hold true to your nonnegotiables, and watch as your life transforms in remarkable ways.

Success Is an Inside Job

A fundamental principle of effective leadership is the understanding that you must first lead yourself before you can effectively lead others. True leadership begins with a deep internal shift that permeates every aspect of your being. The shift occurs when you change your image to that of a leader, raise your Standard for your own actions, develop the attitude that inspires others to follow you, and have the discipline to act consistently with it, day in and day out.

When you cultivate this internal transformation, you will witness a profound shift in your external world.

Everything is an inside out job. The challenges and struggles you face often reflect what is happening within you. By addressing the internal factors that contribute to your difficulties, you gain the power to overcome them and create positive change.

Leading yourself means taking ownership of your actions, thoughts, and beliefs. It requires self-discipline, self-awareness, and self-motivation. It means setting clear goals and developing a plan of action to achieve them. It involves making choices and taking responsibility for the outcomes, learning from setbacks, and persisting in the face of challenges.

As you embark on the journey of self-leadership, it's important to cultivate a mindset of growth and self-improvement. Continuously seek opportunities for personal and professional development. Invest in acquiring new skills, expanding your knowledge, and enhancing your emotional intelligence. Embrace a mindset of curiosity, adaptability, and resilience.

Leadership is not just about commanding or directing others; it's about inspiring and empowering them to reach their fullest potential. By leading yourself, you become a living example of the qualities and values you wish to instill in others. You inspire through your actions, your integrity, and your unwavering commitment to personal growth.

Leading yourself is a vital prerequisite to leading others effectively. By focusing on the internal shift and embracing the inside out approach, you unleash your power to transform your external world.

Recognize the difference between a want and a goal, and channel your emotions and desires into purposeful action. Take ownership of your journey, develop self-discipline, and commit to ongoing growth.

> As you lead yourself with authenticity and intention, you will inspire and lead others to new heights of success.

Embrace Failure as Part of the Process

Failure is an integral part of the journey to success. Every day, I acknowledge and embrace my failures, knowing that they propel me forward without diminishing my confidence. This recognition is one of life's greatest secrets. Fear serves as feedback, providing valuable insights into my inner landscape. I understand that in order to grow, I must develop a strong relationship with failure. Embracing failure signifies a willingness to venture into unexplored territories, surpassing the boundaries most people are unwilling to cross.

Each failure becomes an opportunity for growth. I learn from my mistakes, adjust my approach, and try again. Through this process of perseverance, I eventually reach a breakthrough. Failure becomes not an obstacle, but a stepping stone towards success.

Throughout this journey, it is vital never to lose the sense of enthusiasm that drives me. Living inside out means living with passion, staying connected to the core of my being, and remaining true to my authentic self. It means approaching life with unwavering energy and excitement, regardless of the circumstances.

In the past, I allowed external circumstances to dictate my emotional state. When things were going well, I felt high, and when faced with setbacks, I experienced lows. However, I have come to understand that circumstances do not define my inner state. I choose to detach my emotions from external events and maintain a sense of equanimity and inner peace. This resilience empowers me to overcome failures and setbacks with grace and determination.

A key to success lies in cultivating a resolute attitude: I know what I want, and I have a clear sense of direction. Even if the path I envisioned doesn't unfold precisely as planned, I remain steadfast in my belief that I will ultimately reach my destination. I understand that setbacks and detours are merely temporary deviations, and I trust that there are multiple paths leading to my desired outcome. With this mindset, I am willing to play to win, embracing the risks and challenges that come my way, rather than playing it safe and settling for mediocrity.

Bring Out Your Inner DAWG!

Many people are afraid about what other people think of them. Don't do that! That is a fear that holds you back. Just like being afraid to fail, being afraid that others won't approve of your actions can cause you to settle for less than the life you deserve.

Instead, really bring out your DAWG! Don't worry what other people are thinking.

A DAWG is someone who knows exactly what they want, exactly where they are going, and doesn't let anyone stop them. They have their head down and, through persistence and drive, go for their goals.

We each have a DAWG. It's an instinctual action. It's not intellectual. Let the DAWG out; you're playing to win. It's the IDGAF muscle (as in "I don't give a f—k"). It's not for other people. When you have that going for you, you're going to be the best version of yourself. No one who wants to conform will live at their highest Standard.

When it comes to pursuing our goals and dreams, it's crucial to unleash our inner DAWG. Don't concern yourself with what others may think or say. Embrace your DAWG! It's all about instinctual action, tapping into that primal drive within you. It's not about overthinking or analyzing, but about tapping into your raw potential.

Allowing your DAWG to come to the forefront means playing to win. It's about going all in and giving it your absolute best.

It's about embracing a mindset of determination, resilience, and unwavering focus. When you let your DAWG out, you tap into a fierce energy that propels you forward and pushes you beyond your perceived limits.

The key to fully embracing your DAWG is activating the IDGAF muscle. This doesn't mean being indifferent or disrespectful to others. It means letting go of fear of judgment and external opinions. It means trusting your instincts and taking bold actions without worrying about what others may think. When you operate from this place, you tap into a level of authenticity and freedom that allows you to be the best version of yourself.

Bringing out your DAWG is not about impressing or proving yourself to others. It's about embracing your unique strengths, talents, and passions. It's about living life on your own terms and pursuing your own definition of success. By fully embodying your DAWG!, you elevate yourself to a higher Standard of living, far beyond the limitations of conformity.

Society often encourages conformity, urging you to fit into predefined molds and expectations. However, those who conform rarely reach their full potential. When you embrace your DAWG, you rise above societal norms and limitations. You become a force to be reckoned with, blazing your own trail and leaving an indelible mark on the world.

How can you bring out your DAWG? It starts with self-belief and embracing your unique qualities. Take the time to discover your passions, strengths, and what truly drives you. Trust your instincts and take courageous actions that align with your authentic self. Surround yourself with a supportive network that encourages and celebrates your individuality.

Embracing your DAWG requires practice and consistency. It's about cultivating a mindset of fearlessness and resilience. Don't be discouraged by setbacks or criticisms. Stay focused on your own journey and keep pushing forward, unwavering in your pursuit of greatness.

Don't hold back. Bring out your DAWG Embrace your instinctive action, tap into your IDGAF muscle, and unleash the best version of yourself. Don't be swayed by the opinions of others or the pressures to conform. When you fully embrace your DAWG, you elevate your life to the highest Standard. So go forth with confidence, passion, and the unwavering belief in your own power. Let your DAWG out and conquer the world.

Fear and Faith Reside in the Same House

Fear and faith reside within the same house, occupying different floors. While fear may be more visible and is often ingrained in our upbringing, I choose to shift my perspective towards faith, because I have learned that faith is the catalyst for achieving my goals. Every remarkable achievement I have experienced has required a leap of faith, an unwavering belief that no matter the obstacles, I will do whatever it takes to succeed. Whether I fail or not, I am committed to pursuing my goals with a resolute attitude, knowing deep within that I will ultimately achieve them.

Take a moment now to reflect on something amazing you have achieved in the past.
Did it require a tremendous leap of faith?
Did you demonstrate unwavering commitment and determination, regardless of the challenges?
Embrace the attitude that propelled you during that experience. Let it fuel your present and future endeavors.

Failure is an essential component of the journey towards success. By embracing failure, learning from it, and persisting in the face of adversity, we pave the way for breakthroughs. Living inside out means approaching life with enthusiasm, detached from external circumstances. It involves cultivating a resilient attitude and unwavering faith in our goals.

Recognizing the coexistence of fear and faith, we choose to embody faith and allow it to guide us toward our desired outcomes. Embrace failure, live inside out, and propel yourself towards the extraordinary life you envision.

◄▬▬▮ In the next chapter, we'll talk about the third pillar of a World-Class Wealth Mindset, and that's Attitude. But first go to the appendix and fill out worksheet 3.

5

Attitude
The Key to Unlocking a
Life of Limitless Possibilities

"What changed?" Rachael's coach sat back in his chair, pen in hand. "What made the difference in your career?"

For as long as she could remember, Rachael wanted to be a professional dancer. From her elementary school plays to being on the dance team in high school, to majoring in dance at her university, Rachel took all the right actions to make a good living as a dancer.

But something was stuck. Sure, she had consistent gigs, but was never able to break through to the financial and career success that she'd dreamed of.

"What changed was my attitude," she said with conviction.

"Tell me more," the coach said, smiling.

"I realized that I had always associated being a dancer with being broke. Plus, there weren't any dark-skinned dancers with a, well, thick physique like mine. So I never really saw myself as being able to succeed at the level I wanted."

"How did you change your attitude?" the coach asked.

"I started to own it all. Every time I slept in instead of going to the studio, every time I joined my friends for pizza and beer instead of looking at my body as an instrument that needed care and proper fuel, every time I took an action that wasn't in harmony with what I said I wanted—I owned it. I started to realize that even if there weren't any dancers like me out there, I could

be a role model for all those little girls who were just like me and thought they could never do it. In short, I changed my attitude and got my shit together."

The coach laughed and asked, "What happened next?"

Rachael smiled and said, "The floodgates opened. I started spending more time at the studio, learning new moves and perfecting my existing ones. I started to meet more people who helped my career. And I am really proud to say that I'm the lead dancer in our troupe and am finally living the life I always dreamed of."

Attitude is a topic that resonates deeply with me because I firmly believe that it controls everything in our lives. It is the invisible force that operates within us, shaping our thoughts, feelings, and actions. Our Attitude has an enormous impact on every aspect of our lives, influencing our relationships, our achievements, and ultimately, our ability to create the life of our dreams. To truly experience a massive quantum leap and unlock our full potential, we must understand and harness the power of Attitude.

Think from the Goal

The first step in changing Attitude is to start thinking differently. Remember that we have the power to choose our thoughts and that those thoughts go into our subconscious minds without question.

We must shift our mindset to one that sees our goals as already achieved. Everything you want has already been achieved!

By mentally residing in the end result, we begin to act and think as the person who has already attained their desired outcome. We must recognize that the creation process is already complete, and our goals are already here—there is no need to struggle or strive. The key lies in thinking not from the physical senses, but from the depths of the mind. To fully develop this mindset, we must take extreme ownership of everything that has happened in our lives. We must realize that we are both the problem and the solution.

Own Your Future

If we are truly committed to experiencing freedom and building the life of our dreams, we must adopt an attitude of ownership. This is what Rachael did. She looked at her current results and saw them as a reflection of her past actions and thoughts.

We must never let current results dictate our ideas or limit our potential. Instead, we must take a close look at those results, which directly reflect our past actions and thoughts. Results always tell the truth, serving as a guiding compass to show us what adjustments we need to make in our Attitude and approach.

The thoughts we accept into our minds directly influence our subconscious, which in turn generate our feelings, actions, and ultimately, our Attitude. This holistic view of Attitude encompasses our thoughts, feelings, and actions, all working together to shape our experiences and outcomes. Power flows in and through us. We hold the power to choose our thoughts, and in doing so, we shape our feelings and actions, which ultimately shape our results.

The Only Limitations Are Those You Accept

At Voss Coaching Co., we encourage you to embrace the idea of having a limitless attitude. Remove the lid that restricts your mind and potential. Lack and limitation only exist when we open the door for them. By cultivating a mindset of abundance and endless possibilities, we open ourselves up to receive the bountiful rewards life has to offer.

Every experience, both positive and negative, that you have encountered in your past has prepared you for bigger things. Each triumph, every setback, and every adversity has contributed to your growth and resilience. They have equipped you with the strength and wisdom needed to overcome obstacles and embrace the opportunities that lie ahead.

Your Mindset Must Be Stronger than Your Emotions

Your mindset must be stronger than your emotions. Emotions can often sway us, clouding our judgment and hindering our progress. By maintaining a steadfast and empowered mindset, you tap into your innate ability to navigate challenges, overcome setbacks, and persevere in pursuit of your goals. Believe that you already possess everything you need to make your life a resounding success. The power resides within you; it is up to you to unleash it.

Attitude is the key that unlocks a life of limitless possibilities. It shapes our thoughts, feelings, and actions, ultimately determining our outcomes and the life we create. By adopting a mindset that thinks from the end, taking extreme ownership of our lives, and embracing an attitude of ownership, we empower ourselves to transcend limitations and achieve greatness. Embrace a limitless attitude, leave behind the constraints of lack and limitation, and step into a future where big things await.

Acres of Diamonds

The popular "Acres of Diamonds" story emphasizes that you already have everything you need to become successful; it's just a matter of recognizing it.

The story originated from a speech given by Russell H. Conwell, an American writer, lawyer, and minister, which he delivered over 6,000 times during the late nineteenth and early twentieth centuries. The story goes as follows:

In the mid-1800s, there was a farmer named Al Hafed, who lived in India. Al Hafed was content with his life and land until one day he heard stories about vast fortunes being made in diamond mining. The allure of wealth captivated him, and he decided to sell his farm to search for diamonds elsewhere.

Al Hafed embarked on a long, exhausting journey across the globe in pursuit of diamonds. He spent years traveling from one place to another, exploring various diamond-rich regions, but unfortunately, he never discovered any diamonds. Hopeless and penniless, he eventually drowned himself.

Meanwhile, back at Al Hafed's farm, the man who had purchased it came across an interesting rock in the small stream that ran through the property. He admired its beauty and showed it to a visitor. The visitor, who happened to be a seasoned geologist, recognized the rock as a diamond of immense value.

The farm, which Al Hafed had sold for a meager sum, turned out to be one of the most significant diamond mines ever discovered. It became known as the Golconda diamond mine and yielded an abundance of precious stones, including the famous Hope Diamond.

Al Hafed, in his relentless search for diamonds elsewhere, failed to realize the immense wealth that existed right under his own feet. He had sold his farm, the very land that held untold riches, to embark on an elusive quest for something he believed was more valuable. If only he had recognized the potential and the acres of diamonds within his reach, his life would have been entirely different.

"Acres of Diamonds" has become a widely shared and cherished story, inspiring you to find abundance, success, and fulfillment by tapping into the potential within your own life.

The story serves as a powerful reminder to appreciate and explore the opportunities and potential that surround you every day. It encourages you to make the most of your current circumstances, to be aware of the hidden gems that may lie within your own endeavors, relationships, or environments. Instead of always seeking external solutions or greener pastures, the tale encourages you to cultivate gratitude, vision, and the ability to recognize the value of what you already possess.

The Money Quiz

What is your relationship with money? How you perceive and interact with money plays a significant role in shaping your financial reality. Again, it all boils down to one crucial factor: your attitude. Your attitude toward money determines not only your current financial situation but also the possibilities you believe are within your reach.

This quiz will help you gain insights into your current beliefs, attitudes, and behaviors about money. Answer each question honestly, and at the end, you will receive your quiz results, along with some suggestions for improving your relationship with money.

1. How do you feel when you think about money?
   a. Excited and confident.
   b. Anxious and stressed.
   c. Indifferent and neutral.
   d. Unsure and confused.

2. How do you approach financial decisions?
   a. I carefully plan and consider all options.
   b. I tend to avoid making financial decisions.
   c. I make impulsive decisions based on emotions.
   d. I rely on others to make financial decisions for me.

3. How do you view wealth and abundance?
   a. I believe there are unlimited opportunities for wealth.
   b. I feel that wealth is reserved for a select few.
   c. I think wealth is not important in life.
   d. I'm not sure how to achieve wealth and abundance.

4. How do you handle financial setbacks or challenges?
   a. I see them as opportunities for growth and learning.
   b. I feel overwhelmed and discouraged.
   c. I ignore them and hope they will resolve themselves.
   d. I rely on others to help me navigate through them.

5. How do you prioritize saving and investing?
   a. I make it a top priority and consistently save and invest.

b. I struggle to save and invest regularly.

c. I haven't thought much about saving and investing.

d. I leave it to chance and don't have a clear plan.

6. How do you feel about spending money on yourself?

a. I believe it's important to invest in my own well-being.

b. I feel guilty or selfish when I spend money on myself.

c. I rarely spend money on myself; I prioritize others.

d. I'm unsure about the balance between spending on myself and others.

7. How do you talk about money with others?

a. I am open and comfortable discussing money matters.

b. I avoid discussing money; it makes me uncomfortable.

c. Money is not a topic of conversation for me.

d. I rely on others to handle money discussions.

8. How do you define financial success?

a. Having financial freedom and security.

b. Accumulating material possessions and wealth.

c. Not worrying about money and living a simple life.

d. I'm not sure what financial success means to me.

Now tally up your answers and find out your quiz results.

Mostly A's. Congratulations! You have a positive and healthy relationship with money. You are proactive, financially responsible, and have a growth mindset when it comes to wealth. Keep up the good work, and continue to build on your financial success.

Mostly B's. Your relationship with money may be causing stress and anxiety. It's essential to examine your beliefs and attitudes towards money and work on developing a more positive mindset. Seek financial education and resources to improve your financial confidence and decision-making skills.

Mostly C's. Money may not be a significant focus for you, but it's essential to understand its role in your life. Consider exploring your financial goals and how money can support your well-being and future aspirations. Developing a healthy relationship with money can bring more stability and freedom.

Mostly D's. You seem to have some uncertainties and confusion regarding money. It's crucial to educate yourself, seek guidance, and clarify your financial goals. Developing a clear understanding of money management and adopting positive financial habits can lead to a healthier relationship with money.

Remember, this quiz provides general insights; it's always beneficial to consult with financial professionals for personalized advice. Use the results as a starting point for self-reflection and growth in your relationship with money.

What Is a Scarcity Mindset?

Many people have a scarcity mindset. They believe that money is a limited resource that must be fiercely pursued and protected. This mindset creates a constant state of worry, anxiety, and a feeling of never having enough. When our relationship with money is driven by scarcity, we inadvertently restrict our potential for financial abundance and hinder our ability to thrive.

Operating from a scarcity mindset limits our perspective and narrows our focus down to mere survival. Instead of embracing opportunities for growth and expansion, we become fixated on holding on to what we have, fearful of losing it. Our financial aspirations and dreams remain distant and elusive, as we remain trapped in a cycle of perpetual lack.

It is essential to recognize that money is not inherently scarce. The world is abundant, and opportunities for financial success and prosperity are abundant as well. In every economy, whether there is a recession or a depression, there are people who thrive financially. There are people who experience freedom. They don't give in to fear or a scarcity mindset. They consciously choose their thoughts to create a World-Class Wealth Mindset.

The World-Class Wealth Mindset

Shifting our mindset from scarcity to abundance opens us up to a broader range of possibilities.

When we adopt a World-Class Wealth Mindset, we begin to see money as a flowing and renewable resource. We acknowledge that there is enough for everyone and that our financial success does not come at the expense of others. This mindset frees us from the grip of fear and scarcity, allowing us to embrace a more expansive and positive relationship with money.

By shifting our perspective and embracing abundance, we open ourselves to new avenues of growth and financial well-being. We can focus on creating value, exploring innovative ideas, and seizing opportunities for advancement. Rather than clinging to what we have, we become open to receiving and attracting wealth in many forms.

In cultivating a World-Class Wealth Mindset, we also cultivate gratitude and appreciation for the resources we already have. We shift our attention from what we lack to what we are blessed with, fostering a sense of contentment and fulfillment in the present moment. This mindset shift allows us to make sound financial decisions, invest wisely, and create a positive impact on our lives and the lives of others.

Remember, our relationship with money is not fixed but can be transformed through conscious effort and mindset shifts. By embracing abundance and releasing scarcity, we can break free from limitations and step into a world of financial possibilities and true prosperity.

Our attitude toward money is not fixed or predetermined. We have the power to reshape our beliefs and perceptions, opening ourselves up to a world of abundance and limitless possibilities.

Our relationship with money is deeply intertwined with our Attitude. By cultivating a positive money mindset, embracing abundance, and taking conscious actions to support our financial goals, we open ourselves up to a world of limitless possibilities.

You have the power to reshape your beliefs and perceptions about money. Embrace an attitude of abundance, gratitude, and conscious financial stewardship, and watch as your financial reality transforms, paving the way for a life of true wealth and fulfillment.

The True Test of Positive Mental Attitude

It is often said that it's easy to maintain a positive mental attitude when everything is going well in life; the true test of resilience and growth lies in the ability to maintain that attitude when faced with challenges and setbacks. During times of difficulty, a positive mindset becomes even more crucial, setting apart the amateurs from the professionals in life.

A negative mental attitude, characterized by worry, doubt, and fear, can be a formidable barrier to progress and success. It clouds judgment, drains energy, and hampers the ability to navigate through tough situations. When we allow negative thoughts and emotions to dominate our mindset, we become trapped in a cycle of self-sabotage, hindering our personal and professional growth.

On the other hand, a positive mental attitude empowers us to rise above adversity, transform setbacks into opportunities, and navigate through the toughest of circumstances with grace and resilience. It is the foundation upon which successful people build their lives and careers. But cultivating and maintaining a positive mental attitude in challenging times requires dedication, self-awareness, and a commitment to personal growth.

One of the first steps in developing a positive mental attitude is recognizing the negative thought patterns and self-limiting beliefs that may be holding us back. We must become aware of the worries, doubts, and fears that surface when faced with obstacles or failures. By acknowledging these negative emotions, we can consciously choose to reframe our perspective and shift our focus toward positive possibilities.

A key aspect of maintaining a positive mental attitude during difficult times is practicing self-compassion and resilience. It is essential to recognize that setbacks and failures are a natural part of life's journey; they do not define our worth or potential. Instead of dwelling on what went wrong, we can choose to view these experiences as opportunities for growth and learning. By adopting a growth mindset, we embrace the belief that every challenge presents an opportunity for personal development and eventual success.

Another powerful tool in cultivating a positive mental attitude is gratitude. Expressing gratitude for the blessings and lessons in our lives shifts our attention away from what is going wrong and redirects it towards what is going right. By focusing on the positive aspects of our lives, we develop a broader perspective that allows us to find silver linings even in the darkest of clouds.

Additionally, surrounding ourselves with a supportive network of like-minded people can enhance our ability to maintain a positive mental attitude. By seeking out positive influences, whether through friendships, mentors, or communities, we gain valuable support, encouragement, and inspiration. These associations can remind us that we are not alone in our struggles and that we can maintain a positive mindset even in adversity.

Having a positive mental attitude does not mean denying or suppressing negative emotions. Rather, it entails a realistic acknowledgment of the challenges we face, coupled with an unwavering belief in our ability to overcome them. By allowing ourselves to experience and process negative emotions, we create space for growth, resilience, and ultimately more profound personal and professional fulfillment.

While it may be easy to maintain a positive mental attitude when things are going well, it is during difficult times that such an attitude truly shines. By shifting our perspective, practicing self-compassion and gratitude, seeking support, and embracing challenges as opportunities for growth, we can develop the resilience and mindset necessary to navigate through life's obstacles with grace and determination. It is in the face of adversity that the true professionals emerge, demonstrating unwavering positivity and inspiring others to do the same.

Attitude plays a significant role in our ability to exercise self-control and maintain discipline in our lives. It serves as the gateway to unlocking our inner strength and harnessing our power to make intentional choices and stay committed to our goals. By cultivating a positive and determined attitude, we can navigate challenges, resist temptations, and achieve long-term success.

Self-Control and Discipline

Self-control and discipline are crucial elements in maintaining a positive attitude. They require us to make decisions that align with our long-term objectives, even when faced with immediate gratifications or distractions. Our attitude empowers us to resist the allure of instant pleasures and stay focused on what truly matters in the bigger picture. When we cultivate a mindset of perseverance and determination, we are able to override momentary impulses and make choices that contribute to our well-being and success.

Self-control and discipline are not necessarily innate in us, but they can be developed and strengthened through consistent effort and practice. We can let go of the belief that self-control is limited or fixed, understanding instead that it can be expanded through conscious choice and consistent action. With a determined attitude, we are more likely to persevere through difficult times, knowing that each setback brings us closer to our ultimate goals. We embrace the belief that success is not a linear path but a journey filled with ups and downs, and our attitude becomes the driving force that keeps us moving forward.

Self-Awareness

Cultivating self-control and discipline requires self-awareness and the ability to consciously monitor our thoughts, emotions, and actions.

By observing our attitudes in different situations, we can identify patterns and triggers that may hinder or facilitate our self-control efforts. We can then intentionally shift our attitude towards a more positive and determined mindset, reinforcing our commitment to self-discipline.

Attitude serves as the foundation for self-control and discipline. Cultivating a positive and determined mindset empowers us to make intentional choices, resist immediate gratification, and stay committed to our long-term goals. A proactive Attitude helps us view setbacks as opportunities for growth, maintain resilience in the face of challenges, and develop a growth mindset that supports our journey towards self-improvement. With the right Attitude, we can unlock our inner strength, navigate obstacles, and achieve personal and professional success.

◀▦ In the next chapter, we'll talk about the final pillar: Discipline. But first, go to the appendix and complete worksheet 4.

6

Discipline

In 1982, a young Michael Jordan was far from being recognized as the best player on his University of North Carolina basketball team. As a teenager, he faced the challenges familiar to many students, having to rely on his mother for stamps and spending money. However, even at this early stage of his career, Jordan exhibited a burning ambition and a commitment to greatness, as depicted in ESPN's documentary series The Last Dance.

While the documentary primarily focuses on the Chicago Bulls' historic 1997–98 season, it also sheds light on Jordan's formative years, starting from his freshman season in college. Arriving at UNC without fanfare, Jordan displayed an unwavering determination and work ethic. In an interview featured in the documentary, legendary coach Dean Smith acknowledged that Jordan was inconsistent as a freshman but recognized his fierce competitiveness and his relentless drive to improve.

Jordan made it clear to his coaches, including Roy Williams, who was then an assistant coach at UNC and later the head basketball coach, that he aspired to be the greatest basketball player ever to represent the university. In a powerful exchange, Jordan assured Williams that he had already worked as hard as anyone on his high-school team. Williams challenged Jordan, advising him that achieving such a lofty goal would require an even greater level of dedication and hard work. Although initially taken aback, Jordan responded with determination, making a promise that left an indelible mark on Williams: "I'm going to show you. Nobody will ever work as hard as I work."

This exchange captured the essence of Michael Jordan's character and set the stage for his extraordinary journey in basketball. It revealed his unwavering commitment to pushing beyond perceived limitations and surpassing expectations. Jordan's relentless desire to be the best would define him throughout his career, propelling him to unprecedented heights and cementing his legacy as one of the greatest athletes of all time.

Discipline Takes You to the Finish Line

Michael Jordan is a classic example of a person who was so self-disciplined that success was practically inevitable. He was the one out there practicing free throws when the other players were partying. He was willing to get intravenous fluids in the locker room during halftime when he played while having the flu. There was nothing he wouldn't do to achieve his goals.

Even though you're probably not aiming to be a professional basketball player, you need to adopt the same attitude and mindset. The athletes that are in the top physical and mental condition are the ones who win. We are mental athletes, and we need to condition ourselves to think only what we want to think.

Discipline is the remarkable capacity to issue a command to yourself and follow through with unwavering determination. It embodies the strength to set clear intentions and take decisive action, regardless of obstacles or distractions. Discipline gives you the power to prioritize your goals and stay committed to the tasks necessary to achieve them.

The essence of discipline lies in the ability to overcome the resistance that often accompanies the pursuit of long-term objectives. It requires the courage to confront the inner voice of resistance or temptation and choose the path that aligns with one's vision and values. Discipline empowers you to resist instant gratification and remain focused on the greater purpose.

Discipline is a fundamental pillar of personal growth and success. It allows individuals to develop consistent habits and routines that propel them forward, even when faced with challenges or setbacks. Through discipline, people can cultivate self-mastery, harness their potential, and unlock their true capabilities.

Discipline extends beyond mere self-control: it encompasses commitment, perseverance, and resilience. It involves the willingness to make sacrifices in the present to secure a better future. With discipline, individuals can embrace delayed gratification and prioritize long-term fulfillment over immediate desires.

Discipline is a profound inner strength that empowers individuals to take charge of their lives. It enables them to transcend limitations, break through barriers, and achieve their highest aspirations. By cultivating discipline, individuals unlock the remarkable potential within themselves and set the stage for extraordinary personal growth and achievement.

The Dream Is the First Step

Dreaming about what you want is the first step towards manifesting your desires, but discipline transforms those dreams into reality. Discipline acts as the bridge that connects your goals with the actions necessary to bring them to fruition.

When you dream about what you want, you envision a future filled with possibilities and opportunities. It is the fuel that ignites your passion and sets your intentions in motion. However, without discipline, those dreams may remain wishes, never translating into tangible results.

Discipline provides the structure and focus needed to turn your dreams into actionable steps. It involves setting clear goals, creating a plan, and then diligently following through with the necessary actions. Discipline requires you to stay committed to the long-term vision, even when immediate gratification may seem more enticing.

By cultivating discipline, you develop the habit of taking consistent, purposeful action towards your dreams. It becomes a daily practice of self-mastery and self-accountability. You build resilience and the ability to persevere through challenges, setbacks, and moments of doubt.

Discipline also fosters personal growth and self-confidence. As you consistently work towards your goals, overcoming obstacles and achieving milestones, you develop a sense of achievement and empowerment. Each small step forward reinforces your belief in your abilities and strengthens your resolve to continue.

Dreaming about what you want is the spark that ignites your aspirations, but discipline provides the structure, focus, and determination necessary to transform those dreams into tangible results. By cultivating discipline, you take ownership of your journey, embrace the necessary actions, and bring your dreams to life.

> Ninety-seven percent of people spend their time thinking about what they don't want.

Discipline comes from focusing your thoughts first. Then action follows.

Nobody with bad habits is financially free.

Discipline Your Thinking

Don't let your emotions distract you from what needs to be done. Control your emotions so that they don't control you. By asserting control over your emotions and maintaining focus on what needs to be done, you can navigate the challenges that come your way and stay on top of your mind.

Discipline is the force within you that drives your actions and decisions. It is a conscious choice to direct your energy towards your goals, values, and principles rather than being swayed by external events or the opinions of others. When you resolve not to be defined by outcomes, you free yourself from the constraints of external validation and embrace a sense of inner strength and autonomy. By separating your sense of self-worth from external achievements or failures, you maintain a grounded perspective and a deep understanding of your value. You recognize that your worthiness is not determined by external validation but by your character, integrity, and the choices you make. This mindset allows you to approach challenges and setbacks with resilience and determination, knowing that they do not define you.

Control Your Emotions

Emotional mastery is another crucial aspect of exercising discipline. Although emotions are a natural part of the human experience, it is essential to avoid being controlled by them. Instead, by consciously observing and managing them, you can respond to situations with clarity and wisdom. This allows you to make rational decisions based on your values and priorities rather than being driven by impulsive reactions.

Controlling your emotions does not mean suppressing or denying them. It means acknowledging and understanding them while choosing how to respond in a constructive and balanced manner. This requires self-awareness, self-regulation, and the ability to shift your perspective when necessary. By cultivating emotional intelligence, you can navigate challenges with a calm and focused mind, enabling yourself to stay aligned with your goals and values.

By having discipline and refusing to be defined by outcomes or controlled by emotions, you reclaim your agency and become the master of your own destiny. You embody resilience, inner strength, and a steadfast commitment to personal growth and fulfillment. Through this intentional approach, you transcend external influences and chart a course guided by your authentic self.

If we don't discipline ourselves, the world will do it for us. The world will make a coward out of the undisciplined individual.

Stop Living Outside In

When you don't discipline your thinking, you're living "outside in," and it affects every aspect of your life.

Living outside in refers to a state where your thoughts and actions are primarily driven by external factors. Your mindset and behavior are reactive rather than proactive, and you constantly respond to external stimuli without deliberate intention or alignment with your values and goals.

Discipline of your thinking is crucial for shaping your perception of the world and influencing your own actions and outcomes. When you neglect to exercise control over your thoughts, you inadvertently allow external circumstances, opinions, and events to dictate your internal state and influence your behavior. You become susceptible to external influences, such as what society expects of you, what other people want you to do or not do, or negative circumstances. You become susceptible to what you see in the media, the opinions of others, or anything outside yourself that leads you to disregard your goals.

The consequences of living outside in can be far-reaching. Your decision-making may become impulsive, because you are driven by external validation or short-term gratification rather than thoughtful consideration of your long-term goals and values. You can fall back into old patterns and habits. You may find yourself pursuing paths that are not aligned with your true desires and passions. You might even lower your Standard, which can then affect your self-image. It's like putting your forward momentum into reverse.

Constantly seeking external validation or basing your self-worth on others' opinions leaves you vulnerable to external circumstances. When obstacles appear, you start to feel that you have no ability to change or influence them.

Living Inside Out

On the other hand, when you have discipline in your thinking, you live "inside out." Here you are consciously choosing your thoughts and rejecting any that are not in harmony with your values and goals. Those thoughts go into your subconscious and, when powered by emotion, become the beliefs and actions that create a World-Class Wealth Mindset.

Disciplining your thinking involves being aware of the thoughts that arise, challenging negative or limiting beliefs, and consciously directing your focus towards empowering and positive perspectives. It requires self-reflection, mindfulness, and the willingness to question and reframe unhelpful thought patterns.

By disciplining your thinking, you regain control over your life and create a solid foundation for personal growth and success. You align your thoughts with your authentic self, enabling you to make choices that are in alignment with your values, aspirations, and long-term goals. This cultivates a sense of inner harmony, purpose, and resilience, as you become less influenced by external circumstances and more grounded in your own truth.

Start playing hardball with yourself,
and develop toughness. Do *hard* better.
That comes with discipline.

The Discipline Quiz

What can you do with an unwavering level of discipline? How would your life look, and what could you achieve?

Read each question and choose the option that best represents your response. At the end of the quiz, you will receive your results, indicating the potential outcomes of having discipline in your life.

1. How do you typically approach tasks or projects?
   a. I often procrastinate and struggle to stay focused.
   b. I start with enthusiasm but lose momentum along the way.

     c. I consistently stay committed and follow through until completion.

2. How do you handle distractions or temptations that arise while you are working towards a goal?
   a. I easily give in to distractions and lose track of my priorities.
   b. I occasionally get sidetracked but can refocus after some time.
   c. I am highly disciplined and can resist distractions to stay on track.

3. How consistent are you in maintaining daily habits or routines?
   a. I frequently break my habits or routines and struggle with consistency.
   b. I can be consistent for a while, but then I lose motivation and fall off track.
   c. I am dedicated to my daily habits and routines, rarely deviating from them.

4. How do you handle setbacks or obstacles that come your way?
   a. I often get discouraged and give up easily when faced with challenges.
   b. I may feel temporarily discouraged but can bounce back with effort.
   c. I persevere through setbacks and use them as opportunities for growth.

5. How do you prioritize your time and manage your schedule?
   a. I struggle to prioritize effectively and often feel overwhelmed.
   b. I have some level of organization but find it challenging to stick to my schedule.
   c. I have a clear system for prioritizing tasks and managing my time effectively.

6. How do you approach long-term goals or projects?
   a. I tend to lose interest or motivation before I can achieve significant progress.
   b. I make progress but often get sidetracked or abandon goals halfway through.
   c. I maintain focus and work diligently until I accomplish my long-term goals.

7. How do you respond to commitments or obligations you have made to others?
   a. I frequently struggle to meet commitments and may disappoint others.
   b. I make an effort to fulfill my commitments but occasionally fall short.
   c. I consistently follow through on my commitments and can be relied upon.

8. How well do you manage your finances and save money?
   a. I struggle with financial discipline and often overspend or live beyond my means.
   b. I make some attempts to save money but find it challenging to be consistent.
   c. I am disciplined in managing my finances, saving regularly, and living within my means.

Now tally up your answers and find out your quiz results.

Mostly A's. Developing a higher level of discipline could transform your life. With unwavering discipline, you can overcome challenges, stay focused on your goals, and achieve remarkable success. Cultivating discipline will require dedicated effort and a commitment to personal growth.

Mostly B's. You have some level of discipline, but there is room for improvement. With a stronger commitment, you can elevate your achievements and experience greater fulfillment. Focus on building consistent habits and overcoming obstacles to reach your full potential.

Mostly C's. Congratulations! You already possess a high level of discipline, which greatly enhances your success and personal growth. Your disciplined approach allows you to stay focused, persevere through challenges, and achieve remarkable outcomes. Continue nurturing and harnessing your discipline to reach even greater heights.

This quiz is designed for the purposes of entertainment and self-reflection. The results are not definitive assessments of your level of discipline, although they can provide insights.

Hope Gives You Options

If you find yourself reading these words with doubt, hoping for a different outcome this time, I understand your hesitation. I was in that very position. There was a time when I studied this material for three long years, hoping for change, but nothing changed. It seemed that no matter how much knowledge I accumulated, it made little impact on my life.

Everything started to change when I made a critical shift in my approach. Rather than just absorbing the information, I committed myself to taking consistent action. I took the principles that I'm teaching you in this book and put them into action, weaving them into the habits of my daily life. It was then that I started to live a world-class life.

Knowledge alone is not enough. True change occurs in the application of that knowledge with the practical steps we take. The insights and strategies shared within these pages are meant to be more than theories and concepts; they are meant to be lived and experienced.

By engaging in the practices outlined in this book, you will unlock the hidden potential within you. The seeds of transformation are sown through consistent action and intentional application. As you embrace and implement these principles, you will experience the remarkable shift that has eluded you in the past.

Let go of any doubts and hesitations. Trust in the process and embrace the journey ahead. As you put these principles into practice, you will see remarkable results unfold. The time for action is now.

Discipline Your Attention

The law of focus says that what we focus our attention on grows. This powerful principle reminds us of the impact of attention on our experience and the results in our lives.

Focus acts as a magnet, drawing in more of what we direct our attention towards. When we consistently give our time, energy, and thoughts to a particular area of our lives—be it relationships, career, personal growth, or any other aspect—we naturally attract more of that into our reality. It's like shining a spotlight on a specific area, making it more visible.

If we focus on positive thoughts, opportunities, and possibilities, we create a mindset that is conducive to growth and abundance. By directing our attention to the things we want to cultivate and expand, we align ourselves with the energy and vibration of those desires. This focused mindset enables us to recognize and seize opportunities that align with our goals, attracting more of what we desire.

If we continually focus on negative thoughts, limitations, and challenges, we unintentionally amplify those aspects of our reality. Our attention becomes fixated on problems, obstacles, and what is lacking, which perpetuates a cycle of negativity and limitation. Our mindset becomes clouded with doubt, fear, and scarcity, hindering our ability to see possibilities and solutions.

The law of focus invites us to become intentional and deliberate in directing our attention and energy towards what we want to create and experience. It requires us to cultivate self-awareness and consciously choose where we place our focus. By consistently nurturing positive thoughts, affirmations, and beliefs aligned with our desires, we create fertile ground for growth and expansion.

To apply the law of focus effectively, it is essential to clarify our goals, values, and aspirations. When we have a clear vision of what we want to achieve or experience, we can channel our focus towards those objectives. This involves setting specific intentions, creating action plans, and consistently taking steps that align with them. We also need to be mindful of our thoughts, emotions, and the narratives we tell ourselves to ensure that they support our desired outcomes.

The law of focus works hand in hand with the law of attraction. By focusing on what we want and expanding our awareness around it, we enhance our ability to attract and manifest those desires into our reality. It empowers us to take control of our experiences, shape our reality, and create a life filled with purpose, fulfillment, and abundance.

Double-Binding Messages

You have a choice. You are choosing what you want or what you don't want.

Ask yourself, "Am I sending out a double-binding message?" That is, are you focusing on the results of past actions? If so, you are transferring worry, doubt, and fear back into your subconscious mind and will continue to create the same outcome.

Instead, discipline your mind to focus on what you *do* want, not on what you presently see.

Tell yourself, "I'm creating a life of freedom." Focus on what you're building. Constantly originate the idea that *you are the person who is at your goal.* If you constantly focus on what you are becoming, you will become that. If you constantly focus on the fact you don't see it yet, you will keep your old problems.

Act from the Goal Already Achieved

Act from the goal already achieved. You are creating a mental rehearsal. How does a person who makes $100,000 a month act and think? Discipline yourself to think and act like that person. Take massive action each day.

Be prepared to do what you don't want to do. Get out of your comfort zone. This is how you raise your Image, your Standard, and your Attitude, and change your program to that of one of success.

The time to act is right now—when the emotion is strong. Don't have it be *someday*. Do it *today*. You tap into your life force by combining your goal with an elevated state of energy.

In part 1, we explored the Stick Person and how the conscious thoughts we choose enter the subconscious mind unquestioned, leading in turn to the actions we take.

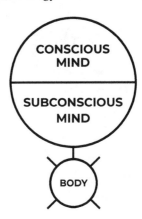

◀▬▬▮ In part 2, we'll take what we've learned about the four pillars and put them into action. But first go to the appendix and complete worksheet 5.

PART TWO

The World-Class Wealth Mindset in Action

7

Image in Action

Terrence Scott woke up in a cold sweat. This was the day he'd been hoping for and also dreading for six months. It was the day he was moving from his hometown in Lebanon, Ohio, to San Francisco to start his dream job. He was leaving everyone he knew and loved behind, putting all of his belongings in a moving truck, and driving 2,400 miles to start a new life.

Was he scared? Yes! However, over the past few months, Terrence had been working on his Image. Every morning he asked himself, "What would a person who lived in San Francisco and worked in Silicon Valley be doing right now? Would he be sleeping in and watching mindless television? Or would he be riding a bike every morning and learning new technology?"

After months of this practice, Terrence began to shift his Image to one that was in harmony with his new life, and the job applications he'd been sending out started getting responses. He'd shifted his program and his self-image and now was embarking on his next adventure.

You no doubt hold dreams of achieving success, landing your dream job, or accomplishing specific goals. Yet not everyone will reach these destinations, not because they can't, but because they never see themselves as the kind of person who could be successful.

Build a Bigger Idea of Yourself

Each person possesses a belief system that has been ingrained in them through influences such as parents, family, culture, values, society, or religion. These beliefs shape our habits, and a collection of habits forms what we call a *program*. Programs help us learn, communicate, and function within society. But they are not always beneficial, and they can operate as negative forces. (For instance, some may hold the belief that only highly educated people can attain financial success.) The only way to progress is by changing our belief systems, thereby transforming our programs. Yet because programs are deeply ingrained, they can be challenging to change.

One major program that lies within each of us is the self-image. Deep within our subconscious mind, an image of ourselves has been formed, shaped by both genetic and environmental factors. This self-image encompasses aspects such as our perception of our physical appearance, our mannerisms, how we think, walk, talk, dress, act, perform, the environments we choose, and even our income. It is tightly intertwined with our self-worth.

The self-image holds immense power in helping us achieve our desires or keeping us stuck in discomfort. It represents how we perceive ourselves based on our actions, choices, experiences, and emotional responses. It encompasses how we feel about ourselves and how we believe others see us.

Sometimes the desire for external validation can override everything else. Many people spend their time managing how others perceive them—their appearance, behavior, and possessions—hoping to gain approval from others. When they do, they often neglect to check if their decisions align with their own true desires and authentic selves. Unbeknownst to them, this habit has taken over their lives, wreaking havoc on their emotional well-being and self-confidence. Instead of considering their own needs, they default to thoughts like:

- What would my family want me to do in this situation?
- Which dress would my partner like the most?

- Which car would make my friends jealous?
- Which career would please my parents?

This constant focus on meeting others' expectations often leads to a tiresome existence. It creates an inauthentic and unhappy life, where there is no space left for the real self. If our self-image is in an unhealthy state, we can easily fall victim to constantly bouncing between various "shoulds" imposed upon us.

An externally focused self-image can pose challenges in the workplace, particularly for leaders and senior managers. For these individuals in particular, it is crucial to maintain a clear focus on the strategic direction of the organization without allowing daily emotional responses, feedback, or perceived expectations to influence their self-image.

What is your self-image based on? Is it primarily influenced by others' opinions and the need to please them? Does it truly reflect how you feel about yourself and what you want for yourself?

If you feel that your current self-image may not be in harmony with the vision you have for yourself, it's essential to embark on a process of self-reflection and self-reassessment. Consider the following steps to update and enhance your self-image:

Self-reflection. Reflect on how you currently perceive yourself. What are your beliefs about your abilities, worth, and potential? Are any self-limiting beliefs or negative self-talk holding you back? Identify areas where you may need to make changes or updates.

Self-awareness. Observe your actions, behaviors, and responses in various situations. Pay attention to how you show up in different areas of your life, such as relationships, work, and personal goals. Be honest with yourself about areas where you can improve and expand.

Personal development. Engage in activities that foster personal growth and development. This can include reading books, attending workshops or seminars, seeking out mentors or coaches, and learning new skills. By investing in your personal development, you can enhance your self-image and expand your capabilities.

Embrace change. Be open to making changes when needed. Recognize that growth and expansion often require stepping out of your comfort zone and embracing new challenges. Seek out opportunities to learn, adapt, and evolve as you work towards your goals.

Positive affirmations and visualization. Utilize positive affirmations and visualization techniques to reinforce a positive self-image. Affirmations are positive statements that reflect your desired self-image, such as "I am capable and worthy of success," "I embrace challenges as opportunities for growth," or "I believe in my ability to achieve my goals." Regularly visualize yourself embodying the qualities, behaviors, and achievements you aspire to.

Surround yourself with supportive influences. Surround yourself with those who uplift and support your growth. Seek out mentors, friends, or communities that inspire and encourage you to reach your full potential. Avoid negative influences or environments that undermine your self-image.

Reflect on each of these points, paying close attention to the self-image you have constructed in your mind. Consider the limitations imposed by this self-image. Do you genuinely resonate with this version of yourself? Are there aspects you would like to change?

 To help you reconnect with your true self-image instead of constantly molding it for others, here's an exercise:

Write down your responses to the following.

1. How do you want others to perceive you? If you could magically determine everyone else's thoughts about

you, what would you want them to think? Consider thoughts like, "That person is so inspiring."

2. Begin by writing a detailed description of the person you currently perceive yourself to be.
3. Construct a new, comprehensive script depicting the person you aspire to become. Consider their appearance, style of dress, self-talk, lifestyle, and sources of joy.
4. Envision this script repeatedly in your mind, immersing yourself in vivid details and allowing yourself to feel the essence of this new version of you.
5. Embrace and embody this script. Read it regularly, visualize it vividly, and integrate it into your daily life.
6. Establish one actionable step per week that will propel you closer to the person you envision.

Now is the time to recreate your self-image by transforming the narrative in your mind, shaping how you present yourself to both yourself and others. Your current reality is a direct manifestation of the self-image you hold, and if you are dissatisfied with your outcomes, it is imperative to alter your thoughts. You must engage your mind in a purposeful manner and actively choose to embody the person you aspire to be.

Fuse with the Essence of Who You Want to Become

This process involves commanding yourself to think, act, and live as the fullest expression of the person you desire to become. This person already exists within you; all you need to do is unlock your potential. I assure you that you possess this power.

Now rewrite the story of the new you, embracing the essence of who you want to become and embodying that individual fully.

1. Write down in the present tense, "I am so happy and grateful now that every day I am getting better and better." Be specific about your

goals. If you want to earn $100,000 a month, for example, write out, "I am so happy and grateful now that I earn $100,000 per month."

2. Read your affirmations aloud every day. Record them on your phone and listen to them ten times a day.

3. Visualize your new self-image. See yourself already there.

4. Watch your self-talk.

5. Act as if you're already the person you want to become.

6. Avoid being influenced by the opinions of other people.

If you do this exercise every day for thirty days, you *will* change your life. The results will blow you away.

Repetition and Emotional Involvement

The power of repetition, combined with emotional involvement, will catalyze a quantum leap in your life. When you consistently engage with your desires and envision yourself in the desired outcomes, you activate a powerful force within yourself that propels you towards those goals.

Repetition plays a crucial role in rewiring the subconscious mind. As we repeatedly focus our thoughts, emotions, and actions on what we want to achieve, we establish new neural pathways that reinforce our desired beliefs and behaviors. This process gradually replaces old patterns and limitations with empowering ones, aligning our subconscious mind with our conscious intentions.

However, repetition alone is not enough: emotional involvement gives it true power. When we emotionally connect with our desires, we ignite a deep sense of passion, motivation, and purpose. This fuels our determination to persist even in the face of setbacks. Emotion acts as the driving force behind our actions, amplifying our focus and energy to move us toward our goals.

As we repeatedly immerse ourselves in the emotional experience of our desired outcomes, we activate the law of attraction. The law of attraction states that like attracts like, and by aligning our thoughts, emotions, and actions with what we want, we draw those experiences and opportunities towards us. By consistently visualizing and feeling the reality of our desired outcomes, we generate a magnetic pull that brings us closer to their manifestation.

Repeatedly involving ourselves emotionally in our desired image also strengthens our belief in ourselves and in the possibility of achieving what we want. As we consistently reinforce the mental and emotional image of success, we cultivate a deep sense of self-confidence and self-belief. This unwavering belief in ourselves and our abilities becomes a powerful driving force that propels us forward, even in the face of uncertainty or adversity.

Emotionally connecting with our desired image helps to reprogram the subconscious mind. As we've discussed, the subconscious mind operates based on deeply ingrained beliefs and perceptions, and by consistently presenting it with a new, empowering image, we reshape its programming. Over time, the subconscious begins to align with this new image, transforming our thoughts, behaviors, and ultimately our results. Through this process, we generate the momentum, confidence, and alignment necessary to manifest our desired outcomes.

Creating a quantum leap in our lives requires more than just repetition and emotional involvement. It also necessitates taking inspired action and embracing opportunities that come our way. Repetition and emotional connection serve as catalysts for aligning our mindset and energy with our goals, but action brings those goals into tangible reality.

Creating a powerful self-image requires consistent self-awareness, self-reflection, and intentional action. By continually updating and expanding your self-image, you can cultivate a positive mindset, enhance your confidence, and unlock your potential to achieve greater success and fulfillment in life.

◄===▮ In the next chapter, we'll go into how to raise your Standard. But first, complete worksheet 6.

8

Standard in Action

Tiffany glanced in the rearview mirror of her Nissan Versa as she pulled into the parking lot of her job at the university. Her eyes were swollen from crying most of the night, but she also saw a steely resolve in them. Glancing at the envelope on the passenger seat of the car, she took a deep breath and said out loud, "I deserve better than this."

The previous day marked her one-year anniversary as the director of marketing for a private college. It was a startup, and she'd taken the job as a favor to a friend, whose dad was trying to launch a new business school. "We can't offer you much more than minimum wage to start. But in a year we should have enough capital to give you a raise." So Tiffany had done double duty as receptionist/secretary and marketing director, knowing that it would pay off. Soon she'd be able to afford a Tesla, like the other cars in the parking lot.

Earlier that week, Tiffany had spent hours preparing a performance evaluation demonstrating that she'd brought in new students, cut expenses, and had launched a successful marketing campaign. Satisfied that her year of hard work would result in the promised raise, she asked for a meeting with her boss.

"Richard, here are some spreadsheets and graphs that show the impact my performance had made over the past year. I'm looking forward to receiving your promised raise."

"Tiffany, I appreciate your contribution over the past year. Your efforts have been noticed. I do need to tell you, though, that we'll be bringing in someone else to take over your role as director

of marketing. We'll keep you on in your current role as receptionist, but I'm afraid that position doesn't warrant a raise. Let's revisit this again in six months, OK?" He set the folder aside and turned his back to her.

Devastated, Tiffany cried the whole way home. "He never intended to make me the director of marketing. He just wanted a glorified secretary to do marketing for minimum wage." By the time she got home, she knew what she needed to do. The letter of resignation was sealed and on the passenger seat of the Versa. "I will not accept working for someone who doesn't value and respect me, ever again. I refuse."

Raising Your Standards

Every one of us has a level in life that we are willing to accept. We might settle for looking less than our best or making less money than we deserve. Nevertheless, in order to create a quantum shift in our lives, we have to raise our Standard. We have to stop accepting anything less than we deserve.

But in order to have something we've never had before, we must be willing to embark on new actions we've never taken before.

True growth occurs at the edges, from stepping out of our comfort zones, rather than from the safety of the sidelines. Unfortunately, when we attempt to break free from our perceived limitations and make different choices, our brain resists change to maintain familiarity and stability.

Positive change often comes with discomfort, and there are no shortcuts for avoiding it. Beware of those who claim otherwise.

Our previous programming keeps us trapped in patterns that no longer serve us, bound by outdated programs. This book provides an opportunity to free yourself from these limiting beliefs and create quantum change.

Yet it's not a simple journey.

We face immense pressure, both externally and internally, to stay the same. Almost everything in our life influences us to stay the same. "Who do you think you are?" we ask ourselves.

We are told—or tell ourselves—that starting a business or achieving financial prosperity is not within our reach, that our bodies are fixed in their current state, and that toxic relationships are our only option.

But it doesn't have to be this way.

We have the power to shift our programs and thereby transform our lives.

Critics argue that teachers of this mindset oversimplify the process, using terms like "manifesting" and "abundance" without any practical application. Sweeping statements like "Anyone can become wealthy!" attract more attention than realistic, measured assertions such as, "With persistent, intelligent effort over an extended period, you can significantly improve your life." I do believe that anyone can get wealthy, but not without raising their Standard. We can never outearn our Standard.

Ordinary Thinking Won't Create World-Class Results

Ordinary thinking and programming won't enable us to achieve something extraordinary. Sustained, massive action, building a successful business, nurturing deep and healthy relationships, or making substantial changes to our bodies is not comfortable. However, it is possible. To accomplish this, we must consistently reinforce the mental vision of who we are becoming. We need to gather evidence of our desired state, persisting until our subconscious programming aligns with this new reality, acknowledging that this is our true identity and what we deserve.

This approach is far different from merely reciting positive affirmations in the mirror and expecting instant results. Affirmations are important, but they aren't enough. True change only begins to happen when they spark a program shift.

Raising our standards requires changing our program, which can be likened to an internal thermostat that determines what we believe we deserve. Understanding this is vital: The external circumstances of our lives will align with the level to which our internal thermostat is set. Living at level 100 is impossible if our thermostat is set at 75. We must raise our standards and refuse to settle for anything less than a level 100 life.

But once we set our thermostat to, let's say, level 85, mental forces like anxiety, self-doubt, and impostor syndrome will attempt to pull it back down to 75. It takes diligent effort to elevate our thermostat, moving from 76 to 77 and beyond. It's not an easy task, and many people falter and give up.

But the effort is always worthwhile. Changing our program, elevating our standards, and continually raising our internal thermostat can yield long-lasting results, even over a lifetime.

Conversely, if we quit and never try again, the effects of inaction will persist indefinitely

What Are You Afraid Of?

Here are some common fears that many people experience:

- Fear of failure
- Fear of change
- Fear of success
- Fear of money
- Fear of disapproval
- Fear of rejection
- Fear of losing control

Reflect on the fears that hold you back in life. Reflect on whether these fears are grounded in reality or if they are products of your imagination. Make a list of the things you fear. Be honest with yourself! Then, next to it, make a note of whether or not the fear is real or imagined.

Run toward Your Fears

Sometimes we may require external help to help us overcome fear. Engaging in physical activities, such as dancing in your living room, listening to comedy, or playing uplifting music can be helpful. Nature, animals, or spending time with children can also provide solace. It's important to avoid relying on food, alcohol, or drugs to cope with fear. Remember to be compassionate toward yourself when fears arise. Acknowledge them and swiftly get back on track, just like hopping back on a bicycle and pedaling forward. The longer we remain motionless, the stronger the grip of fear becomes, prolonging the paralysis.

Fear does not have to overpower us; it only does so if we grant it power. Refuse to let fear overpower you. Instead, focus on calming down rather than slowing down. Do not compromise your dreams in exchange for fear. Recognize its presence and continue moving forward. This requires practice and concentration. You can visualize yourself triumphantly surpassing fear and achieving victory. Successful people often employ vision boards as aids in this process.

Belief Systems

Now let's examine your belief system. Is it holding you back?

Take a few moments to reflect on your own belief system. Identify any thoughts or beliefs that may be impeding your progress. Consider whether these perceived limitations are based on reality or if they exist solely in your imagination. For instance, you might believe that others view you as less competent or talented than you perceive yourself to be. Is this belief grounded in reality, or is it merely a product of your imagination?

Belief systems play a crucial role in shaping our thoughts, actions, and overall mindset. They can either empower us to achieve our goals or hold us back from reaching our full potential. This quiz will help you assess whether your current belief system is supporting your growth or acting as a hindrance. Be honest with yourself while answering the following questions. At the end, you will receive your results and some insights to help you explore and shift your beliefs if necessary.

?

Quiz: Is Your Belief System Holding You Back?

1. How often do you catch yourself thinking negatively about your abilities or potential?
   a. Rarely or never.
   b. Occasionally.
   c. Frequently.

2. When faced with a new challenge, what is your immediate reaction?
   a. I see it as an opportunity for growth and success.
   b. I feel uncertain and doubt my ability to handle it.
   c. I assume I won't be able to overcome it

3. Do you believe that you have the power to change your circumstances and create the life you desire?
   a. Absolutely; I believe in my ability to shape my reality.
   b. I'm not sure, but I hope it's possible.
   c. No, I believe external factors determine my outcomes.

4. How often do you compare yourself to others and feel inadequate?
   a. Rarely or never.
   b. Occasionally.
   c. Frequently.

5. When facing setbacks or failures, how do you interpret them?
   a. I see them as valuable learning experiences and opportunities to improve.
   b. I tend to blame myself and feel discouraged.
   c. I see them as proof that I'm not capable of succeeding

6. How much do you believe in your own potential for growth and development?
   a. I strongly believe in my capacity to grow and learn.
   b. I have some doubts, but I'm open to the idea of personal growth.
   c. I doubt my ability to change or improve significantly.

7. How often do you take risks or step outside of your comfort zone?
   a. Frequently; I believe that growth happens outside of comfort zones.
   b. Occasionally, but I often hesitate or feel apprehensive.
   c. Rarely; I prefer to stay within my comfort zone

8. Do you believe that failure is an essential part of the learning and growth process?
   a. Yes, I embrace failure as a stepping stone to success.
   b. I'm not sure, but I try to learn from my failures.
   c. No, I see failure as a sign of personal inadequacy

9. How much influence do you think your mindset has on your overall success and happiness?
   a. A significant amount; I believe mindset is a key determinant of success.
   b. I think mindset plays a role, but it's not the sole factor.
   c. I don't believe mindset has much impact on outcomes.

10. Are you open to challenging and questioning your existing beliefs?
    a. Absolutely. I actively seek new perspectives and challenge my beliefs.
    b. I'm open to it, but I sometimes struggle with letting go of old beliefs.
    c. No, I'm resistant to changing my beliefs and prefer to stick to what I already know.

Count the number of times you selected each option. Which was the most common one?

Mostly A's. Your belief system is generally empowering and supportive of your growth. You have a positive mindset that propels you forward and allows you to overcome challenges effectively.

Mostly B's. Your belief system may have some limitations or doubts that can hold you back at times. Consider exploring and challenging these beliefs to unlock your full potential.

Mostly C's. Your belief system appears to be holding you back from reaching your full potential. It's important to examine and challenge these limiting beliefs to create a more empowering and supportive belief system.

Beliefs can be reshaped with conscious effort and self-reflection. Embrace the opportunity to explore new beliefs that align with your goals and aspirations, and always remember that you have the power to shape your own reality.

You may encounter real limitations that you can't control. In this case, you need to shift your focus away from them. For the things that are real limitations that you *can* control, act to change them. Use the power of conscious thought to reject limitations that are merely imagined.

How to Raise Your Standard

Raising your Standard is a powerful way to improve various aspects of your life and achieve greater success. Here are some strategies to help:

Clarify your values and priorities. Reflect on what truly matters to you in different areas of your life, such as relationships, career, health, and personal growth. Identify the values and principles that you want to uphold, and use them as a foundation for setting higher standards.

Set specific and challenging goals. Establish clear and measurable goals that align with your values and aspirations. Make sure these goals push you outside of your comfort zone and require you to stretch and grow. Ambitious goals naturally raise your standards to match the level of achievement you desire.

Surround yourself with high achievers. The people you surround yourself with have a significant impact on your mindset and standards. Seek out individuals who have already achieved the level of success you aspire to and who embody the qualities and behaviors you want to emulate. Their presence and influence can inspire you to raise your own standards.

Continuous learning and personal development. Commit to ongoing learning and personal growth. Invest in your knowledge and skills by reading books, attending seminars, taking courses, or seeking mentors. By continually expanding your knowledge and improving yourself, you raise your standards and become more capable of achieving your goals.

Take consistent action. Standards are not just about thoughts and intentions; they require consistent action. Develop discipline and a strong work ethic to consistently take action towards your goals. Challenge yourself to maintain a high level of commitment, consistency, and perseverance even when faced with obstacles or setbacks.

Evaluate and adjust. Regularly assess your progress and evaluate whether your current standards are still serving you. Be open to adjusting and raising your standards as you grow and evolve. Learn from your experiences, celebrate your successes, and identify areas where you can raise the bar even higher.

Embrace discomfort and failure. Raising your standards often involves stepping outside of your comfort zone and taking calculated risks. Embrace discomfort and be willing to face challenges and failures along the way. See them as opportunities for growth and learning rather than as signs of inadequacy. Embracing discomfort and failure allows you to continually push your limits and raise your standards.

Raising your standards is a gradual process that requires consistent effort and self-reflection, so be patient with yourself while staying committed to continual improvement. As you raise your standards, you'll experience personal growth, increased fulfillment, and a greater sense of achievement.

Get emotionally involved with getting outside your comfort zone.

9

Attitude in Action

Once upon a time, in a small town nestled between rolling hills and lush forests, there lived a man named Alex. He was known for being exceptionally frugal and cautious with his money. Growing up in a humble family, he learned early on the value of thriftiness and saving every penny. However, this approach to money had its drawbacks, as it prevented him from experiencing the joys of life and forming meaningful relationships.

As the years passed, Alex became more and more obsessed with accumulating wealth. He would turn down invitations from friends to go out and have fun, citing financial concerns. He was afraid of spending money on anything that wasn't strictly necessary, fearing that any unforeseen expenses might disrupt his carefully planned budget.

One day, as Alex was walking through the town's market square, he noticed a crowd gathered around a street performer. The performer was an elderly man who played the violin with such passion and skill that the melody seemed to touch the hearts of everyone within earshot. People were smiling, clapping, and throwing coins into the performer's open violin case.

Alex was captivated by the music but felt a pang of guilt at the sight of others parting with their hard-earned money so freely. He decided to approach the old musician after his performance, curious to understand why he relied on the generosity of strangers.

The violinist, whose name was Mr. Lawrence, welcomed Alex with a warm smile. He explained that many years ago, he used to live a life similar to Alex's, focused solely on money and material possessions. However, a life-altering event made him reevaluate his priorities.

"I was once like you, young man," Mr. Lawrence began. "Always worrying about money, never taking time to enjoy the beauty around me. Then one day, I lost everything in a terrible fire. All my possessions, all my savings—gone in an instant."

Alex listened intently, moved by the musician's story.

"At first, it was devastating," Mr. Lawrence continued, "but it made me realize that life isn't just about accumulating wealth. It's about experiences, connections, and sharing our talents with others. Money is important, but it should never be our sole focus."

The old man's words struck a chord with Alex. He started attending Mr. Lawrence's performances regularly, slowly allowing himself to enjoy the music and the sense of community that surrounded the street shows.

Over time, Alex's attitude toward money began to shift. He still valued financial security, but he learned to appreciate the balance between saving for the future and living in the present. He started accepting invitations from friends, spending time with them, and making memories that enriched his life.

As Alex's perspective on money evolved, so did his social circle. He became more open, approachable, and compassionate. People noticed the change in him, and he found himself forming meaningful relationships with others in the town.

One day, Alex came across a local charity that helped underprivileged children gain access to education and basic necessities. He was moved by the cause and decided to contribute some of his savings to support the organization. The act of giving brought him a sense of fulfillment that he had never experienced before.

As the years passed, Alex struck a harmonious balance between financial responsibility and enjoying life's offerings. He still managed his money wisely but no longer let it control every aspect of his life. Instead, he allowed himself to be generous, not just with his finances but also with his time and emotions.

People admired the transformation in Alex, and he became an inspiration for others in the town. Mr. Lawrence's lessons stayed with him, reminding him always that money was a tool to be used wisely, not an end in itself.

Alex's story spread far and wide, inspiring countless others to reevaluate their attitudes toward money and find a healthier, more fulfilling way to live. As he continued to embrace life with an open heart, his journey became a testament to the transformative power of changing one's attitude about money.

You Have an Attitude towards Money

To transform our relationship with money, we must first examine our existing beliefs and thought patterns. Are we conditioned to believe that money is hard to come by? Do we associate money with stress, greed, or negative connotations? These deep-seated beliefs can act as subconscious barriers, preventing us from fully embracing the abundance that is available to us.

Once we become aware of these limiting beliefs, we can consciously choose to adopt a new attitude—one that is rooted in abundance, gratitude, and a growth mindset. Instead of viewing money as a scarce resource, we can shift our perspective and see it as a tool for creating positive change in our lives and the lives of others. By cultivating an attitude of abundance, we recognize that there is more than enough wealth and prosperity to go around.

Changing our attitude toward money requires a fundamental shift in our thoughts, feelings, and actions. We must actively engage in practices that support a positive money mindset. This may involve affirmations, visualizations, or gratitude exercises that help rewire our subconscious mind to focus on abundance rather than scarcity. By consistently reinforcing positive beliefs about money, we invite new opportunities and experiences into our financial realm.

It is crucial to develop a healthy relationship with money—one that is grounded in conscious spending, wise investing, and responsible financial management. This means understanding our financial goals, creating a budget, and making informed decisions about how we earn, save, and invest our money. By taking control of our finances and becoming active participants in our financial journey, we empower ourselves to manifest the financial abundance we desire.

You Can Have a Lot of Money and Still Not Be Wealthy

Wealth encompasses more than mere monetary value: it includes health, relationships, personal growth, and a sense of purpose and fulfillment. By expanding our definition of wealth, we shift our focus from solely accumulating money to creating a well-rounded and prosperous life.

Here are some universal laws that govern money and the World-Class Wealth Mindset.

The Law of Compensation

The law of compensation is based on three factors:
1. The need for what you do.
2. Your ability to do it.
3. The difficulty of replacing you.

The law of compensation says that you are compensated in direct proportion to the value you bring to others or to society. People who provide greater value, whether in terms of skills, knowledge, products, or services, are more likely to receive higher compensation than those who offer less. By delivering exceptional value, continually improving, and positively affecting others, you can align yourself with this law and increase your chances of receiving abundant compensation in various forms.

The law of compensation operates on the premise of fairness and balance. It suggests that people who make significant contributions will receive corresponding rewards in return. Conversely, those who offer little value or contribute negatively may experience fewer rewards or face negative consequences.

Compensation can take various forms, such as financial rewards, recognition, opportunities, or personal fulfillment. Like wealth itself, the law of compensation is not limited to money alone. It also encompasses nonmonetary forms, such as personal growth, satisfaction, and fulfillment.

The law of compensation encourages you to focus on developing your skills, talents, and abilities to provide greater value to others. By continually enhancing your knowledge, honing your skills, and improving your offerings, you can increase your compensation and create more opportunities for success and abundance.

This law does not guarantee immediate or direct correlation between effort and reward, because external factors and circumstances may intervene. However, over time, when you consistently deliver value and contribute positively, you are more likely to attract greater opportunities, recognition, and rewards.

The Impression of Increase

The "impression of increase" is a powerful principle that encourages leaving a positive impact on the people and environments we interact with. It embodies the idea of striving to make everyone better off than they were before their interaction with us.

When we embrace the mindset of leaving an impression of increase, we seek opportunities to uplift, support, and enhance the lives of others. It goes beyond mere transactions or exchanges; it is about making a lasting, positive difference in your surroundings.

By embodying this principle, we become agents of positive change. We bring kindness, compassion, and empathy into our interactions, seeking to understand others, acknowledge their needs, and contribute to their well-being. This principle can be applied in various aspects of life, including personal relationships, professional settings, and community engagements.

In personal relationships, the impression of increase means being present for others, listening actively, and offering support and encouragement. It involves nurturing relationships, fostering growth, and helping others unlock their full potential. Whether it's lending a listening ear, offering a helping hand, or sharing knowledge and resources, the goal is to leave a positive and lasting impact on the lives of those we care about.

In the professional realm, the impression of increase translates into going above and beyond in our work. It means striving for excellence, delivering exceptional results, and making valuable contributions to the organization and its stakeholders. By adding value to our work and collaborating effectively with colleagues, we create an environment of growth and success that benefits everyone involved.

On a broader scale, the impression of increase extends to our communities and the world at large. It entails taking responsibility for our actions, being mindful of our impact on the environment, and contributing to the betterment of society. It can involve volunteering, supporting charitable causes, advocating for social justice, or promoting sustainability. Through these actions, we leave a positive imprint on our communities, making them stronger, more inclusive, and more vibrant.

Ultimately, the impression of increase is a guiding principle that reminds us of our capacity to make a difference. It encourages us to look beyond our own needs and desires and consider how we can uplift and empower others. By consciously striving to leave everyone better off than we found them, we contribute to a more compassionate, connected, and thriving world.

Service to Many Creates Great Wealth

Service to many creates great wealth. That is, you can achieve abundance and prosperity by providing value to a large number of people.

This principle highlights the connection between service, impact, and financial and personal rewards.

When we focus on serving others, whether through our products, skills, expertise, or acts of kindness, we create opportunities to make a positive impact on a larger scale. By addressing the needs, desires, and challenges of a broader audience, we increase the potential for our offerings to be embraced and valued by a larger number of people.

The concept of wealth extends beyond financial gain. While providing valuable service can lead to financial abundance, it also encompasses a broader definition of wealth, including emotional fulfillment, personal growth, and a sense of purpose. When our efforts contribute to the well-being and success of others, they often lead to a deep sense of satisfaction and a wealth of meaningful connections and relationships.

Creating great wealth through service requires a mindset shift from a transactional approach to a more relational and value-driven perspective. It involves understanding the needs and aspirations of our target audience and finding ways to meet those needs effectively. By continuously improving and refining our offerings, we can provide outstanding value.

This principle also encourages us to explore ways to expand our impact without compromising the quality of our service. This may involve leveraging technology, building teams, or developing systems that allow us to serve a larger number of people efficiently and effectively.

Moreover, this principle acknowledges the inherent interdependence between service and wealth creation. As we contribute to the well-being of others, they in turn are more likely to support us and contribute to our own growth and prosperity. Through positive word of mouth, referrals, and loyal customer relationships, our reputation and influence can grow, leading to increased opportunities and financial rewards.

Ultimately, the principle that service to many creates great wealth reminds us of the power of focusing on others and creating value in their lives. By embracing this mindset and committing to making a positive impact on a larger scale, we open ourselves up to abundance, fulfillment, and meaningful success.

Raise Your Frequency

Another important principle: *raise your frequency to match the frequency of your goals.* In short, we must align our energy, mindset, and actions with our desired outcomes. We must elevate our internal state and vibrational frequency to match the level of our goals.

Every goal or desire carries a specific energetic frequency. Our thoughts, emotions, beliefs, and actions also emit frequencies that create our overall energetic state. When our personal frequency aligns with the frequency of our goals, we create a harmonious resonance that attracts and manifests those goals more easily.

Raising our frequency involves several key elements:

Clarity. Clearly defining our goals and intentions provides a specific direction for our energy and focus. It allows us to channel our thoughts and actions towards the desired outcomes.

Positive mindset. Cultivating a positive and empowering mindset is crucial. By shifting our thoughts and beliefs to ones that support our goals, we create a more uplifting vibrational frequency.

Emotional alignment. Emotions carry powerful energy. Aligning our emotions with the joy, gratitude, and excitement we would feel upon achieving our goals helps us resonate with the frequency of success.

Self-care and well-being. Taking care of our physical, mental, and emotional well-being raises our overall energetic state. This includes practices such as exercise, healthy eating, restful sleep, and stress reduction techniques.

Surroundings and relationships. The people around us and the environments we inhabit can impact our frequency. Surrounding ourselves with positive, supportive individuals and creating a conducive environment for growth and success can elevate our energy.

Action and alignment. Taking inspired action aligned with our goals is essential. It demonstrates our commitment and willingness to move forward. Aligning our actions with our intentions creates momentum and further raises our frequency. In this way, we attune ourselves to a vibrational level that resonates with our goals. This alignment in turn opens the door for synchronicities, opportunities, and the manifestation of our desires. It helps us tap into the universal laws of attraction and abundance.

Raising our frequency requires consistent practice and self-awareness. It involves daily rituals, mindfulness, and intentional choices to align ourselves with our goals. As we continue to raise our frequency, we become more attuned to the possibilities available to us, enhancing our ability to manifest our goals and create a life in alignment with our deepest desires.

10

Discipline in Action

Aiden walked into the gym and headed into the free-weight section. He loved nothing more than having the whole place to himself, and when you belong to a gym that opens at 4:00 a.m., it's easy to do that. As he took a break between sets to run on the treadmill, his phone alerted. He'd gotten another overdraft charge for a bounced debit.

"I don't understand it. I'm so disciplined in every other area of my life. I work out every day, eat clean, don't drink alcohol or do drugs. I got great grades in school and give everything to my job. Why can't I stop going broke?"

Throughout this book, I've been reinforcing the idea that our results don't lie. If we don't like what we're seeing in a certain area of life, it means that something needs to change. The change has to start internally, with a shift in our self-image and our Standard and Attitude. But at some point, we also have to take consistent action in order to effect change externally.

Most of us are familiar with what we need to do to maintain a healthy body: we have to develop a daily routine that involves exercise, healthy eating, water, sleep, stress management, and saying no to anything that isn't in harmony with our health goals.

It's the same thing with wealth. A World-Class Wealth Mindset requires a daily routine that keeps you saying yes to the life you are building.

Daily Disciplines for Wealth

Creating daily disciplines for wealth can help you cultivate habits and practices that support your financial well-being and long-term prosperity. This daily routine should incorporate all of the four pillars you've learned in this book.

Here's a suggested daily routine that can create a World-Class Wealth Mindset:

Morning visualization and affirmations. Start your day by visualizing your financial goals and affirming positive statements about wealth and abundance. Set your intentions for the day, and envision yourself achieving financial success. This practice helps to align your mindset with your goals and sets a positive tone for the day.

Use the power of repetition to state your desired outcome in the present tense throughout the day.

Review financial goals and priorities. Take a few minutes to review your financial goals and priorities. Remind yourself of what you're working towards and the steps needed to achieve it. This helps keep your goals at the forefront of your mind and guides your decision-making throughout the day. Don't allow yourself to focus too much on "what is," but use it as a reminder to stay focused on what you are building.

Money management. Allocate some time to managing your finances every day. Review your budget, track expenses, and update your financial records. Ensure that you're staying within your budgetary limits and making progress towards your savings and investment goals. This practice helps you stay organized and in control of your financial situation.

Continuous learning. Expand your financial knowledge and skills. Read books, articles, or listen to podcasts about personal finance, investing, or wealth-building strategies. Stay informed about economic trends and financial markets. Continuous learning enhances your financial literacy and empowers you to make informed financial decisions.

Daily action steps. Identify at least one action step each day that moves you closer to your financial goals. It could be researching investment opportunities, networking with professionals in your field, or finding ways to increase your income. Consistent action is crucial for long-term wealth creation.

Healthy financial habits. Incorporate healthy financial habits into your routine. This may include automating savings, reviewing and optimizing your investments, and seeking ways to reduce unnecessary expenses. Regularly review your financial habits to ensure they align with your goals and values.

Gratitude practice. Express gratitude for the financial abundance you already have. Cultivating gratitude shifts your mindset towards abundance and attracts more positive experiences. Consider keeping a gratitude journal or taking a few moments each day to reflect on the financial blessings in your life.

Self-care and well-being. Maintaining good physical and mental health improves your ability to focus, make sound financial decisions, and perform at your best. Prioritize exercise, healthy eating, restful sleep, and stress management techniques.

Reflect and evaluate. End your day by reflecting on your financial actions and progress. Evaluate what went well, and identify areas for improvement. Plan adjustments to your financial strategies if needed.

Rest and relaxation. Allow yourself time to unwind and relax. Engage in activities that bring you joy and help you recharge. It's important to find a balance between wealth-building activities and personal fulfillment.

Consistency and commitment are key to building wealth, so aim to integrate these practices into your daily life consistently.

Live from the End

It's easy to fall into a mindset of lack when you're focusing on finances. You may be tempted to cut corners, buy the least expensive item, look for deals and savings, and learn to do without things you really want.

This is the *opposite* of what you should be doing. The world is an abundant place, and you need to focus on finding that abundance. Remember earlier when we talked about the law of focus? There is more than enough money to go around, and you want to live your life from the place as if you were already wealthy.

Does this mean you go out and buy a Porsche with your grocery money? No. But it does mean that you focus on how it would feel to drive your dream car. Don't resent your old car with 100,000 miles on it. Be grateful for it. Focus on what you love about it. Because what we focus on grows.

The $100 Bill Challenge

Go to the ATM and take out a $100 bill. If you can't, take out the largest bill you can afford to withdraw. Keep it in your wallet or purse. As a result, you'll automatically start programming your subconscious mind to accept the idea, "I can afford that," all day long.

The Power of Decision-Making

Here's an exercise: make an irrevocable, committed decision and act on it within thirty seconds.

This powerful practice can propel you towards your goals. Here's a step-by-step guide to help you make and act on such a decision:

1. Identify the decision. Clearly define the decision you want to make. It could be related to a personal goal, a change in behavior, or a significant action you want to take. Ensure that the decision aligns with your values and aspirations.

2. Gather information. If needed, gather any relevant information or insights that will help inform your decision. Assess the potential risks, benefits, and consequences associated with your choice. However, keep in mind that the purpose of this exercise is to act quickly, so don't get caught in analysis paralysis.

3. Set a deadline. Challenge yourself to make the decision within a specific time frame. In this case, aim to make your decision within thirty seconds. Setting a deadline creates a sense of urgency and prevents overthinking.

4. Trust your instincts. In the given timeframe, trust your instincts and intuition to guide you. Sometimes our initial gut reactions hold valuable insights. If you are hesitating, remind yourself of the importance of commitment and taking decisive action.

5. Affirm your decision. Once you've made your decision, affirm it to yourself. Repeat it mentally or aloud to reinforce your commitment. Embrace a mindset of determination and conviction that you will follow through on your decision.

6. Take immediate action. Without delay, take the first step towards implementing your decision. This could be as simple as making a phone call, sending an email, or creating a plan of action. By acting promptly, you establish momentum and demonstrate your commitment to your decision.

7. Embrace responsibility. Hold yourself accountable for your decision. Take ownership of the outcome and be prepared to face any challenges or obstacles that may arise. Remember that true commitment requires perseverance and resilience.

8. Reflect and adjust. After taking action, periodically reflect on the progress and impact of your decision. Assess whether adjustments or refinements are needed along the way. Stay open to learning and adapting as you work towards your desired outcome.

By making irrevocable, committed decisions and acting on them swiftly, you cultivate a mindset of decisiveness and proactivity. This practice can help you overcome indecision, build self-confidence, and propel you towards your goals.

Decision-making is the difference between winning and losing. It plays a crucial role in determining success and failure. Our choices impact our personal and professional lives profoundly.

Effective decision-making provides clarity and focus on our path. It allows us to define our goals, set priorities, and align our actions accordingly. By making thoughtful decisions, we can avoid aimless wandering and instead channel our efforts towards meaningful objectives.

Decisions often involve assessing risks and opportunities. A willingness to make timely decisions enables us to seize opportunities as they arise. Procrastination or indecision can result in missed chances for growth, innovation, and advancement. Taking decisive action puts us in a better position to capitalize on favorable circumstances.

You can't solve problems effectively if you don't know how to make good decisions. And, making good decisions involves evaluating options, considering alternatives, and choosing the best course of action to address challenges. Effective decision-making skills enable us to analyze problems objectively, weigh potential solutions, and make informed choices that lead to desired outcomes. If we don't have a system in place for making good decisions, we fall into all kinds of traps and make decisions that aren't in harmony with our goals.

I tell my clients to do this exercise because the ability to make quick and effective decisions is essential. Decisiveness allows us to adapt to new circumstances, adjust strategies, and navigate uncertainty. By embracing a proactive decision-making mindset, we can respond swiftly to emerging trends, challenges, and opportunities.

Making decisions empowers us to take ownership of our actions and outcomes. When we make a conscious choice, we accept responsibility for its consequences, whether positive or negative. Embracing accountability fosters personal growth, builds trust, and enhances our credibility.

Every decision we make, regardless of the outcome, offers insights and lessons that contribute to our personal and professional development. Reflecting on the results of our decisions allows us to refine our decision-making process and make better choices in the future.

Moreover, making effective decisions strengthens our self-image. It makes others trust us more and want to follow us. Confidence in decision-making enables us to guide and influence others, driving positive change and achieving collective goals.

 Once you make a decision, don't change it lightly.

Changing Your Mind

Once you make a decision, approach any potential changes with careful consideration. While it is natural for circumstances and information to evolve over time, altering a decision should not be taken lightly. Here are a few reasons why it is generally advisable to think twice before changing a decision.

Clarity and conviction. A decision is often the result of thoughtful analysis, weighing options, and considering various factors. Changing a decision lightly may indicate a lack of conviction or clarity. It is crucial to have a solid foundation and strong rationale for any change in decision.

Ripple effects. Decisions have consequences, and altering a decision can set off a chain reaction of adjustments and adaptations. These ripple effects can affect not only the original decision but also other elements and individuals. Changing a decision without considering these implications can lead to confusion, inefficiency, and even mistrust.

Trust and reliability. Consistency and reliability are important traits in personal and professional relationships. When others depend on your decisions, changing them lightly can erode trust and credibility. It is essential to demonstrate consistency in decision-making to foster trust and maintain a sense of reliability.

Time and energy. Making decisions consumes time, energy, and resources. Changing decisions lightly can result in wasted effort, divert attention from other priorities, and disrupt the flow of progress. It is important to evaluate the cost-benefit analysis of changing a decision, considering whether the potential benefits outweigh the costs.

Learning and growth. Sticking to decisions, even when faced with challenges or setbacks, can provide valuable opportunities for learning and growth. It helps develop resilience, problem-solving skills, and adaptability. Changing decisions too readily can limit personal growth and hinder the ability to navigate complex situations.

🔒 Make Decisions from the Goal

Another related principle: the importance of making decisions based on factors beyond immediate results. It's generally unwise to look at something and say, "It's not working. I need to change what I'm doing." You have to have the discipline to stay the course and carry out the decision you chose. Stay committed to the actions that will give you what you want, even if they don't seem to be working at first.

Instead of solely focusing on the end result, shift your attention to the process and the actions required to achieve your goals. Emphasize the quality of your efforts, consistency, and adherence to your values and principles. By giving your best in each step of the journey, you increase your chances of long-term success.

When intermediate results become the sole determinant of your decisions, you may become risk-averse or unwilling to try new approaches. By shifting your mindset and embracing a growth-oriented perspective, you open yourself up to new possibilities and solutions. Emphasize personal growth and continuous improvement, recognizing that setbacks and failures are valuable opportunities for learning and development.

Results can fluctuate in the short term because of factors such as external circumstances and uncontrollable variables. Instead of making decisions solely based on immediate outcomes, take a long-term perspective. Consider the potential future implications of your choices, the alignment with your values and aspirations, and the overall progress you are making towards your goals.

Trust, but Verify

Trust in the process and the effort you are putting in. Understand that success often requires perseverance, resilience, and patience. Avoid making impulsive decisions or changing course solely based on short-term results. Trust that your consistent efforts and commitment to the process will yield positive outcomes in the long run.

While it's essential not to let results solely dictate your decisions, it's still crucial to evaluate your progress and adjust your approach when necessary. Regularly assess your actions, strategies, and outcomes to identify areas for improvement. Use feedback and data to inform your decision-making and make strategic adjustments that align with your long-term goals. In short, trust the process, but verify that you're still on the right path.

The journey toward your goals is at least as important as the destination. It has been said that the true gift of your journey to personal freedom is the gift, not money or possessions.

Embrace the experiences, challenges, and personal growth that occur along the way. By focusing on the process and enjoying the journey, you can derive fulfillment and satisfaction from your efforts, regardless of immediate outcomes.

Remember, decisions driven solely by short-term results can limit your potential and lead to reactive behavior. By maintaining a broader perspective, focusing on the process, and embracing growth and learning, you can make decisions that align with your values, aspirations, and long-term success.

> Discipline is more than a suggestion
> you give yourself.

Discipline goes beyond mere suggestions or intentions. It is a powerful force that requires commitment, consistency, and unwavering dedication.

Commitment. Discipline starts with a strong commitment to your goals and values. It involves making a firm decision to follow through on your intentions, even when faced with challenges or temptations. It requires a deep-rooted dedication to staying focused and taking consistent action.

Consistency. Discipline is about showing up consistently and doing what needs to be done, regardless of whether you feel motivated or not. It involves creating daily routines and habits that align with your goals and sticking to them, even when it feels difficult or inconvenient.

Self-control. Discipline requires self-control and the ability to resist immediate gratification or distractions. It means making choices that serve your long-term goals, even if they require short-term sacrifices or discomfort.

Accountability. Discipline thrives in an environment of accountability. Hold yourself accountable for your actions and progress. This can involve setting deadlines, tracking your performance, seeking feedback, or partnering with someone who can provide support and hold you responsible.

Focus and prioritization. Discipline involves maintaining a laser-like focus on your priorities and avoiding unnecessary distractions. It means saying no to activities or commitments that do not align with your goals, allowing you to direct your energy and attention towards what truly matters.

Overcoming resistance. Discipline requires facing and overcoming resistance, both internal and external. Internal resistance may arise from self-doubt, fear, or limiting beliefs. External resistance can come in the form of obstacles, setbacks, or criticism from others. Discipline enables you to persevere and push through these challenges, remaining steadfast on your path.

Growth and self-development. Discipline is a tool for personal growth and self-development. It involves seeking opportunities to learn, improve, and expand your capabilities. It means continuously pushing yourself beyond your comfort zone and embracing challenges as opportunities.

Integrity and trust. Discipline is built on a foundation of integrity and trust. It means keeping the promises you make to yourself, being honest with your actions and intentions, and staying true to your values. It fosters self-respect and builds trust in your ability to follow through on your commitments.

Ultimately, discipline is a mindset and a way of life. It requires a conscious choice to prioritize your goals, take consistent action, and maintain self-control. By cultivating discipline, you empower yourself to achieve your aspirations, overcome obstacles, and create the life you desire.

Obstacles Are Gifts

We often encounter obstacles that appear to obstruct our path to success. At times, we may feel as if we have reached a dead end, a cul-de-sac, or traffic gridlock along our chosen road. However, a profound Zen proverb reminds us that these obstacles are not roadblocks: they are an intrinsic part of the journey.

Obstacles don't have to halt our progress. We cannot bypass or avoid them; we must confront and overcome them. They are akin to the changing wind in sailing, where we must adjust our sails to continue moving forward. As psychologist Abraham Maslow wisely observed, we are constantly moving either forward into growth or backward into safety. Do we choose to embrace the path of growth or succumb to disintegration by retreating?

When we keep our focus on the horizon, our goals remain within our sight. The only limits we truly face are self-imposed. Consider those who run track with prosthetic lower limbs: they demonstrate the qualities of courage, determination, and imagination necessary to navigate through obstacles.

Inspirational author Neville Goddard once said, "We are only limited by the weakness of our attention and the poverty of our imagination." It takes bravery, inspiration, and unwavering determination to move past the barriers of fear. Obstacles can manifest in various forms, including other people. But along the way, we may encounter some individuals who provide support and act as the wind beneath our wings.

Take a few moments to reflect on the obstacles in your own life. Consider the aspects that hinder your progress. Look at whether these obstacles are tangible or products of your imagination.

In part 2 of this book, we looked at the actions we can take to build on the four pillars. In part 3, we'll take it up to the next level and discover how you can change not only your world but *our* world.

PART THREE

Raising the Global Standard

11

The Attitude of Service

"Pete, you're not listening to me." Pete's wife was standing in front of him with her hands on her hips, and she was angry.

"Yes, I am. You were telling me about your sister and her first day on the job and how she didn't know the Wi-Fi password and couldn't log on for three hours."

"That's not listening; that's repeating back to me what I just said. You may be hearing me, but I can tell you're listening to the game in the other room."

"No, I'm not!" (Yes, he was.)

"Let me ask you. Who is winning?"

"The other team." Pete knew he was in trouble with this line of questioning.

"Now, where does my sister work? What's her new job?"

"Uhhh . . ." Pete knew he was busted. "I'm sorry, honey. You're right. Let me turn off the TV in the next room, and I'll listen and pay attention this time."

What Does It Mean to Serve?

Serving, in its essence, means to contribute to, support, or assist others or a greater cause. It is an act of selflessness and a genuine expression of care, compassion, and empathy. Serving goes beyond mere actions or tasks; it involves a mindset and a heartfelt desire to make a positive difference in the lives of others or the world.

To serve means to prioritize the needs, well-being, and growth of others above one's own self-interest. It is about showing up with a genuine desire to help, uplift, or bring value to others without expecting anything in return. Service can take many forms, whether it's volunteering, mentoring, supporting a cause, or simply being there for someone in need.

Serving is not limited to grand gestures or significant acts. It can manifest in everyday interactions, such as lending a listening ear, offering a kind word, or performing small acts of kindness. It recognizes the inherent interconnectedness of humanity and acknowledges that our actions, no matter how small, can have a profound impact on others.

Serving is also an opportunity for personal growth and self-discovery. It allows us to transcend our individual concerns and connect with something larger than ourselves. By serving others, we develop a sense of purpose, fulfillment, and a deeper understanding of our own potential. It cultivates qualities such as empathy, gratitude, and humility, enhancing our well-being and enriching our relationships.

Serving can extend to serving communities, society, or even the planet. It acknowledges the interconnectedness of all living beings and our responsibility to contribute positively to the collective welfare.

In the end, serving is both a mindset and a way of being in the world. It is about embodying values such as kindness, compassion, and generosity in our thoughts, words, and actions. It offers opportunities to make a meaningful impact, create positive change, and leave a lasting legacy. By embracing the spirit of service, we not only uplift others but also cultivate a sense of purpose, fulfillment, and a more harmonious and compassionate world.

You might be wondering, "Arash, that's all fine and good, but what does this have to do with cultivating a World-Class Wealth Mindset and getting personal freedom? I'm looking to change *my* life, not the whole world."

The fact is, the best way to change your own life is to have an attitude of helping others.

Giving Returns Tenfold

When you give with an attitude of service, it opens up positive possibilities and enriches your own life in various ways. Here are some ways in which giving with a service-oriented attitude can bring about abundant returns:

Deepened connections. Serving others fosters genuine connections and strengthens relationships. When you selflessly give and support others, it creates a sense of trust, appreciation, and gratitude. These deeper connections can lead to lasting friendships, support networks, and opportunities for collaboration.

Personal growth. Serving others provides an avenue for personal growth and self-improvement. By engaging in acts of service, you develop empathy, compassion, and patience. It expands your perspective, broadens your understanding of different experiences, and enhances your interpersonal skills. Through service, you learn valuable lessons, gain new insights, and cultivate a greater sense of self-awareness.

Fulfillment and happiness. Serving others can bring immense joy and fulfillment. When you contribute to the well-being of others, it creates a sense of purpose and meaning in your own life. Witnessing the positive impact of your actions and seeing the gratitude on the faces of those you serve can generate a profound sense of contentment.

Reciprocity and support. Giving with an attitude of service often triggers a ripple effect of kindness and generosity. Others are inspired by your actions and may be inspired to pay it forward, creating a cycle of reciprocity. Additionally, when you are in need, the community you have served may come to your aid and provide support, strengthening the bonds of trust and unity.

Personal and professional opportunities. Serving others opens doors to new opportunities. Your acts of service can showcase your skills, talents, and character, leading to personal and professional growth. It may create networking opportunities, open doors to collaborations, or even lead to career advancements or new ventures. People are often drawn to those who genuinely care and contribute to the well-being of others.

Positive energy and gratitude. Giving with an attitude of service generates positive energy and gratitude within yourself and in the world around you. Focusing on the well-being of others shifts your mindset from scarcity to abundance, from self-centeredness to a more expansive outlook. This positive energy attracts more positivity into your life, fostering a cycle of gratitude and abundance.

Personal satisfaction. Serving others brings a deep sense of personal satisfaction. Knowing that you have made a positive impact on someone's life or contributed to a cause greater than yourself can be incredibly fulfilling. It reaffirms your values, purpose, and the belief that you can make a difference in the world.

The returns you receive from serving others may not always be tangible or immediate. They may come in the form of intangible rewards, personal growth, or the knowledge that you have made a positive difference. Nevertheless, by embracing an attitude of service, you create a positive and abundant mindset that not only benefits others but also brings immeasurable rewards to your own life.

An Attitude of Wealth

One of my favorite stories illustrates how someone who is really wealthy on every level has a different attitude than the people around him. Scott was at a charity event with a bunch of associates. One of the guys at the table was commenting on Scott's choice of wristwatch. It wasn't anything expensive or special: it was just a watch he liked.

"You should get a Rolex, Scott," someone said. "It would make you look rich."

Without wavering, Scott looked at the man directly in the eyes and said, "I am rich. I don't have to look it."

Later that evening, as the charity event went on, the emcee called Scott up to the podium to thank him. Without anyone knowing, Scott had donated several million dollars to this charity, and the whole evening was possible because of his donation.

> People with a World-Class Wealth Mindset don't need to show it off. Instead, they pay it forward.

You Are Directly Rewarded

When you contribute value to others, you often receive direct rewards that align with the significance of your contribution. Here are some ways in which you can be directly rewarded for the value you provide:

Financial compensation. One of the most direct forms of reward is financial compensation. When you deliver value through your products, services, or expertise, people are willing to pay for it. Your clients, customers, or employers recognize the worth of your contribution and compensate you accordingly. This can take the form of a salary, fees, commissions, bonuses, or other monetary benefits.

Increased opportunities. Providing value can open doors to new opportunities. When others witness the impact and quality of your work, they may approach you with collaborations, partnerships, or job offers. These opportunities can lead to personal and professional growth, expanded networks, and access to resources that further enhance your success.

Enhanced reputation and influence. Consistently delivering value builds a positive reputation and increases your influence. As people recognize your expertise and the positive impact you have, they are more likely to trust and seek your guidance or services. Your reputation becomes a valuable asset that attracts new opportunities, referrals, and a wider audience.

Personal and professional growth. Serving others enables you to continually learn and grow. The challenges and experiences encountered in providing value help you develop new skills, expand your knowledge, and improve your abilities. This personal and professional growth contributes to your overall success and positions you for even greater rewards in the future.

Gratitude and recognition. Providing value often elicits gratitude and recognition from those who benefit. People appreciate the positive difference you make in their lives and express their thanks. Their acknowledgment can come in the form of verbal praise, written testimonials, awards, or public recognition. Such expressions of gratitude are rewarding in themselves and fuel your motivation to continue serving others.

Long-term relationships. Delivering value fosters long-lasting relationships with clients, customers, colleagues, and collaborators. These relationships, built on trust, respect, and mutual benefit, can lead to repeat business, ongoing partnerships, and a loyal customer base. Nurturing these relationships becomes a rewarding aspect of your work as you develop meaningful connections and a strong support network.

Personal fulfillment and happiness. Ultimately, the greatest reward for providing value is personal fulfillment and happiness. Knowing that you have improved someone's life, helped them overcome challenges, or contributed to their success brings a deep sense of satisfaction and purpose. This invaluable, intrinsic reward serves as a driving force to continue making a difference.

The Random Acts of Kindness Challenge

To practice developing an attitude of service, take the Random Acts of Kindness Challenge. For the next thirty days, do one act of service for someone else. Here are some ideas, but feel free to come up with your own.

1. Pay for the meal or coffee of the person behind you in line.
2. Send a handwritten thank-you note to someone who has made a difference in your life.
3. Volunteer your time at a local charity or community organization.
4. Offer to help an elderly neighbor with their groceries or household chores.
5. Leave positive and uplifting notes in public places for strangers to find.
6. Donate clothes, books, or household items to a local shelter or thrift store.
7. Offer to babysit for a friend or family member who needs a break.
8. Compliment a stranger and brighten their day.
9. Bring treats or snacks to your coworkers or classmates.
10. Send a care package to a soldier or someone serving overseas.
11. Hold the door open for someone or help someone carry their bags.
12. Offer to walk a friend's dog or pet-sit for a neighbor.
13. Leave a generous tip for a server or service worker.
14. Help someone with their yardwork or gardening.
15. Share your knowledge or skills by offering free tutoring or mentoring.
16. Leave quarters at a laundromat or vending machine for someone to use.
17. Send flowers or a small gift to someone who could use a pick-me-up.
18. Offer to drive a friend to an appointment or run errands for them.
19. Let someone go ahead of you in line at the grocery store.
20. Write a positive online review for a local business you appreciate.

21. Help a student with their schoolwork or offer to proofread their essay.
22. Donate blood or register as an organ donor.
23. Surprise a friend or family member with a homemade meal or baked goods.
24. Share your favorite book or movie with someone and discuss it together.
25. Offer to mentor or support someone who is starting a new venture or project.
26. Leave a generous tip for a street performer or musician.
27. Offer to give a friend or family member a ride to the airport or train station.
28. Leave a kind and encouraging comment on someone's social media post.
29. Offer to teach someone a new skill or hobby that you enjoy.
30. Smile and greet people you encounter throughout the day.

Notice how good you feel and how much fun it is!

Making a great impact is about consistently choosing actions that uplift, support, and inspire those around you. By living with intention and creating positive change, you can make a meaningful difference in the lives of others.

12

Helping Others Create
a World-Class Wealth Mindset

My entire career has been spent in service of learning and then teaching others how to strengthen their mindset. I have used these lessons in my own life and those of the people I've worked with. But I wondered, "How can I serve more people? How can I create something that lasts beyond my lifetime?"

From this attitude of service, I created Voss Coaching Co. with my friend and cofounder Mykie Stiller. We realized that the best way to create a legacy was to help others create a World-Class Wealth Mindset. Now that you know the four pillars, we want you to help spread the word too.

To help others create a World-Class Wealth Mindset, you need to help them master the four pillars of Image, Standard, Attitude, and Discipline. This chapter will give you some ideas and suggestions on how to do that.

Helping Others Elevate Their Image

Helping others improve their self-image is a powerful and transformative act of support. Here are some strategies you can employ to assist others in doing so:

Provide encouragement and validation. Offer genuine and specific compliments to acknowledge others' strengths, talents, and accomplishments. Validate their efforts, and remind them of their unique qualities and capabilities. Encouragement can boost their confidence and reinforce positive self-perception.

Be a supportive listener. Practice active listening and create a safe space for others to express their thoughts, feelings, and concerns. Show empathy and understanding without judgment. Sometimes simply being present and allowing them to share their experiences can help them gain clarity and perspective.

Offer constructive feedback. Provide feedback in a constructive and supportive manner. Focus on highlighting areas of improvement rather than criticizing shortcomings. Help them recognize their potential and guide them towards growth and development. Encourage a growth mindset that embraces challenges and learning opportunities.

Challenge negative self-talk. Help others identify and challenge negative self-talk or beliefs that hold them back. Encourage positive affirmations and help them reframe their thoughts in a more empowering and self-affirming way. Help them recognize their worth and challenge self-doubt.

Encourage self-care and self-reflection. Emphasize the importance of self-care practices, such as maintaining physical health, engaging in hobbies, and prioritizing personal well-being. Encourage self-reflection to foster self-awareness and introspection. Help others identify their strengths, values, and passions, and guide them towards activities that nurture their self-esteem.

Offer resources and support. Share relevant books, articles, podcasts, or workshops that focus on personal development and building self-image. Provide guidance on available resources, mentors, or support groups that can further assist them on their journey of self-improvement.

Be a role model. Lead by example, and demonstrate a positive self-image in your own life. Show confidence, resilience, and self-compassion. Your behavior and attitude can inspire and motivate others to cultivate a healthier self-image.

Celebrate successes. Acknowledge and celebrate others' achievements, no matter how small. Recognize their progress, and reinforce the positive changes they have made. Celebrating successes boosts their confidence and reinforces their belief in their own abilities.

Practice patience and empathy. Changing one's self-image is a gradual process that requires time and patience. Be understanding and compassionate throughout the journey of others. Support them even during setbacks, and remind them that growth and self-improvement are ongoing processes.

Helping Others Raise Their Standard

Helping others raise their Standard involves supporting and empowering them to reach new levels of excellence and achievement. Here are some ways to assist others in this area:

Lead by example. Be a role model and demonstrate high standards in your own life. Show consistency, discipline, and a commitment to personal growth. When others see your dedication and the positive results it brings, they may be inspired to raise their own standards.

Encourage self-reflection. Help them assess their current standards and identify areas where they desire improvement. Encourage them to reflect on their values, goals, and aspirations. Self-reflection allows for a deeper understanding of their current situation and the potential for growth.

Provide support and accountability. Offer support, guidance, and encouragement throughout their journey of raising their standards. Check in regularly to track progress, provide feedback, and hold them accountable for their commitments. Help them stay focused and motivated, especially during challenging times.

Foster a growth mindset. Encourage them to adopt a growth mindset, which embraces challenges, sees failures as learning opportunities, and believes in the potential for personal development. Help them reframe setbacks as temporary obstacles, and encourage resilience and perseverance.

Inspire and motivate. Share stories of those who have successfully raised their standards and achieved remarkable results. Inspire and motivate others through your words and actions. Help you believe in their own potential and create a vision of what is possible.

Helping Others Develop a Winning Attitude

Helping others cultivate a positive mental attitude is a powerful way to support their personal growth and well-being. Here are some strategies for assisting others in this way:

Show your own positive mental attitude. Display optimism, resilience, and gratitude in your thoughts, words, and actions. Your positive energy can inspire and influence others.

Encourage self-awareness. Help others become aware of their current thought patterns and beliefs. Support them in identifying any negative or self-limiting thoughts that may be holding them back. Encourage self-reflection and introspection to help them understand the impact of their thoughts on their emotions and behavior.

Promote positive self-talk. Teach others the importance of positive self-talk. Encourage them to replace negative self-talk with affirming and empowering statements. Help them challenge and reframe negative thoughts into more positive and constructive perspectives.

Support positive surroundings. Help others create an environment that supports positivity. Encourage them to surround themselves with supportive and uplifting people. Suggest engaging in activities and hobbies that bring joy into their lives.

Provide emotional support. Be there to listen and offer emotional support when others face challenges or setbacks. Validate their feelings and provide encouragement. Sometimes simply having someone who understands and empathizes can make a significant difference.

Offer perspective. Help others gain perspective by reframing situations in a more positive light. Assist them in seeing challenges as opportunities for growth and learning. Encourage them to focus on solutions rather than dwelling on problems.

Helping Others Develop Discipline

As we have learned, developing discipline is crucial for personal growth and achieving goals. Here are some ways you can help others develop discipline:

Set clear goals. Encourage them to clearly identify what they want. Clear goals provide a sense of direction and motivation, making it easier to stay disciplined.

Create accountability. Establish accountability measures to help others stay committed to their goals. This can involve regular check-ins, progress tracking, or finding an accountability partner or group. By being accountable to someone else, they are more likely to stay disciplined and follow through on their commitments.

Provide structure and routine. Help others create a structured environment and establish daily routines. A consistent routine helps build discipline by creating habits and reducing the temptation to deviate from the intended path. Encourage them to prioritize their tasks and allocate dedicated time for important activities.

Break tasks into manageable steps. Large or overwhelming tasks can sometimes hinder discipline. Teach others to break tasks into smaller, manageable steps. By focusing on one step at a time, they can make progress without feeling overwhelmed, which boosts motivation and discipline.

Teach time management. Effective time management skills are essential for discipline. Teach others how to prioritize tasks, set deadlines, and manage their time effectively. Encourage them to eliminate distractions and create a conducive work environment to optimize productivity and maintain discipline.

Foster self-accountability. Help others develop self-accountability by encouraging them to take ownership of their actions and choices. Teach them to reflect on their progress, identify areas for improvement, and hold themselves accountable for their commitments. Self-reflection promotes self-discipline and personal growth.

Celebrate progress and milestones. Recognize and celebrate the achievements and milestones others each along their journey. Positive reinforcement boosts motivation and encourages continued discipline. By acknowledging their progress, you help them stay focused and committed to their goals.

Provide support and encouragement. Be a source of support and encouragement for others as they develop discipline. Offer guidance, motivation, and praise for their efforts. Let them know that discipline is a skill that can be learned and improved over time.

Lead by example. Demonstrate discipline in your own life. Be consistent, reliable, and disciplined in your actions and commitments. When others see your disciplined approach, it can inspire and motivate them to develop similar habits.

13

Wealth Beyond Money

Roger lay in his bed, looking out the window at the trees and flowers. He could hear birds chirping and the soft voices of the people in the hall of his hospice. At eighty-five-years old, he was losing his battle with cancer and had come to this place to die comfortably.

Roger had a long career—two of them, actually. In the 1970s he'd started a business with his brother, and they were able to expand to locations around the country. After a full career doing that, he tried to retire, but found himself bored out of his mind and annoying his wife every day. So he started a second career creating and selling handcrafted wood tables. He'd had some success with that as well and was able to live comfortably until his cancer diagnosis the previous year.

Was Roger wealthy? Yes. Financially, he would leave a nice inheritance to his wife and three adult children. His grandchildren would be taken care of. More than that, Roger felt that he was wealthy in ways that were invisible.

His brother Glen had also achieved financial security, but Roger wouldn't call him wealthy. Glen lived a life that was highly leveraged and was spending more money each month than he had coming in. He'd also been married four times, his adult children wanted nothing to do with him, he was profoundly unhealthy (a rich idea coming from a guy with terminal cancer, Roger chuckled), and he had zero spiritual connection.

Roger loved his brother, but was grateful that at the end of his life he himself had true wealth. Not the kind that can be measured in dollars or passed down in a will. Roger had wealth beyond money.

As we approach the end of this book, I want you to pause reading and think about your results. What results came to your mind? Were they your health? Your wealth? Your income? What came to mind? You earned the results you have in your life. If you don't like what you've done, there is still time to change it. For Glen in our story above, he is not on his deathbed, like his brother Roger. He can still make changes.

Things that are free are the most valuable. Health, relationships, spiritual connection—you can't buy those. They are the real wealth in our lives. Wealth beyond money.

We have to unleash the power we have right now instead of waiting until it's too late.

Unleash the Power Five

Here are the Power Five:

1. Decision
2. Image
3. Standard
4. Attitude
5. Discipline

Use the Power Five to build wealth beyond money. Let's look at some ideas you can use to be wealthy in the things you can't buy.

Relationship Wealth

Building relationship wealth involves nurturing and cultivating strong, meaningful connections with others. Here are some ways to develop relationship wealth:

Communication. Effective communication is essential for building and maintaining healthy relationships. Practice active listening, express your thoughts and feelings clearly, and be open to understanding others' perspectives. Clear and respectful communication fosters trust and strengthens relationships.

Trust and honesty. Trust is the foundation of any meaningful relationship. Be trustworthy and maintain honesty in your interactions. Trustworthiness involves keeping promises, being reliable, and maintaining confidentiality. Building trust takes time and consistency.

Empathy and understanding. Show empathy and understanding towards others. Put yourself in their shoes, listen to their experiences, and validate their emotions. Being compassionate and understanding helps create a safe and supportive environment for open communication and deepening connections.

Quality time. Building relationship wealth requires dedicated time and attention. Make it a priority to spend quality time with loved ones, friends, and colleagues. Engage in activities together, have meaningful conversations, and create lasting memories.

Support and encouragement. Be supportive of others' goals, dreams, and aspirations. Offer encouragement, celebrate their successes, and provide assistance when needed. A supportive and uplifting environment enhances relationship wealth by fostering growth and mutual well-being.

Conflict resolution. Conflict is a natural part of any relationship. Learn effective conflict resolution skills, such as active listening, finding common ground, and seeking win-win solutions. Address conflicts openly and honestly, and work towards finding resolutions that strengthen relationships rather than causing further harm.

Appreciation and gratitude. Express appreciation and gratitude for the people in your life. Acknowledge their contributions, show gratitude for their presence, and regularly express your love and care. An attitude of gratitude enhances relationship wealth and creates a positive atmosphere.

Boundaries and respect. Establish healthy boundaries, and respect the boundaries of others. Understand and communicate your needs while being mindful of their boundaries. Respecting personal space, opinions, and choices fosters a sense of safety and respect within relationships.

Mutual growth and support. Encourage personal and professional growth within your relationships. Support each other's goals and aspirations, provide constructive feedback, and help each other learn and develop. The pursuit of growth together strengthens relationship wealth.

Forgiveness and acceptance. Practice forgiveness and acceptance in relationships. Understand that people make mistakes, and holding grudges can hinder relationship growth. Foster an environment of understanding, compassion, and acceptance, allowing room for growth and healing.

Health Wealth

Developing health wealth involves taking proactive steps to prioritize and enhance your physical and mental well-being. Here are some strategies to develop health wealth:

A balanced diet. Focus on consuming a balanced and nutritious diet. Include a variety of fruits, vegetables, whole grains, lean proteins, and healthy fats in your meals. Limit processed foods, sugary drinks, and excessive salt and sugar intake. Consult a healthcare professional or nutritionist for personalized guidance.

Regular exercise. Engage in regular physical activity that suits your fitness level and preferences. Aim for a combination of cardiovascular exercises, strength training, and flexibility exercises. Find activities you enjoy and make them a part of your routine. Consult a fitness professional for guidance if needed.

Adequate sleep. Prioritize quality sleep, and establish a consistent sleep routine. Aim for seven to nine hours of sleep each night. Create a comfortable environment, limit exposure to electronic devices before bedtime, and practice relaxation techniques to promote better sleep.

Stress management. Develop effective stress management techniques to minimize any negative impact on your health. Practice relaxation techniques like deep breathing, meditation, or mindfulness. Engage in activities that bring you joy, such as hobbies, spending time in nature, or engaging in creative outlets.

Regular medical checkups. Schedule regular checkups with healthcare professionals to monitor your health. This includes routine physical examinations, screenings, and preventive care. Address any concerns promptly and follow recommended treatments or therapies.

Mental and emotional well-being. Pay attention to your mental and emotional well-being. Practice self-care activities that promote stress reduction and emotional balance, such as journaling, therapy, or engaging in hobbies. Seek support from loved ones or professionals when needed.

Healthy relationships. Foster healthy relationships that provide support, positivity, and emotional connection. Surround yourself with people who uplift and inspire you. Maintain open communication, express your needs, and seek help when necessary.

Work-life balance. Strive for a healthy work-life balance to avoid burnout and promote well-being. Set boundaries between work and personal life, prioritize self-care, and engage in activities outside of work that bring you joy and relaxation.

Personal growth. Continually work on personal growth and self-improvement. Set goals, learn new skills, and engage in activities that challenge and stimulate your mind. Embrace lifelong learning, and pursue interests or hobbies that contribute to your intellectual well-being.

Positive mindset. Cultivate a positive mindset, and practice self-compassion. Focus on positive self-talk, gratitude, and celebrating your achievements. Surround yourself with positive influences, and engage in activities that promote optimism and a positive outlook.

Spiritual Wealth

Spiritual wealth refers to the abundance and richness that comes from nurturing and developing one's spiritual well-being. It is the state of experiencing a deep sense of connection, purpose, and inner fulfillment. Spiritual wealth goes beyond material possessions and focuses on the growth and expansion of one's spiritual self. It encompasses beliefs, values, practices, and the exploration of meaning and purpose in life.

Here are some elements that contribute to spiritual wealth:

Connection with a higher power or transcendent reality. Spiritual wealth often involves cultivating a connection with a higher power, whether through religious beliefs, meditation, prayer, or similar practices. It is about experiencing a sense of transcendence and recognizing something greater than oneself.

Inner peace and serenity. Spiritual wealth involves finding inner peace and serenity amidst life's challenges and uncertainties. It can be achieved through practices such as mindfulness, meditation, reflection, or spending time in nature. Cultivating a calm and centered state of mind contributes to spiritual well-being.

Values and ethics. Having a strong moral compass and living in alignment with one's values contributes to spiritual wealth. It involves making choices that reflect honesty, integrity, compassion, and empathy towards oneself and others.

Self-reflection and personal growth. Spiritual wealth involves self-reflection, introspection, and self-exploration. It includes a willingness to question beliefs, learn from experiences, and continuously evolve and grow as an individual.

Meaning and purpose. Seeking and discovering meaning and purpose in life is an essential aspect of spiritual wealth. It involves understanding one's unique gifts and passions, and how they contribute to a larger purpose or make a positive impact on the world.

Gratitude and appreciation. Cultivating gratitude and appreciation for the present moment and the blessings in one's life is a significant part of spiritual wealth. It involves recognizing and acknowledging the beauty and abundance that surrounds us.

Compassion and service. Spiritual wealth often includes acts of kindness, compassion, and service. It involves extending love, support, and assistance to those in need, fostering interconnectedness and empathy.

Connection and community. Building connections with like-minded people and participating in a supportive community can contribute to spiritual wealth. It involves engaging in meaningful relationships and shared experiences that nurture spiritual growth and understanding.

Acceptance and letting go. Spiritual wealth involves embracing acceptance and letting go of attachment to outcomes, past regrets, or negative emotions. It is about surrendering to the flow of life and finding peace in the present moment.

Transcending the ego. Spiritual wealth includes transcending the ego's limitations and cultivating a sense of unity with all beings as well as with the inherent divinity and interconnectedness of all life.

Mental Wealth

Mental wealth refers to the state of having a healthy and flourishing mind. It encompasses emotional resilience, cognitive abilities, psychological health, and overall psychological flourishing. Mental wealth goes beyond the absence of mental illness; instead it is a matter of nurturing and developing positive mental states and qualities.

Here are some key elements that contribute to mental wealth:

Emotional resilience. Emotional resilience is the ability to bounce back from setbacks, cope with stress, and adapt to challenging situations. It includes skills such as emotional regulation, self-awareness, and the ability to manage and navigate a range of emotions effectively.

Positive mindset. Cultivating a positive mindset is an important aspect of mental wealth. It involves adopting an optimistic outlook, focusing on strengths and possibilities, and maintaining a positive attitude towards oneself and life's circumstances. Positive thinking can enhance well-being and lead to greater mental wealth.

Self-acceptance and self-compassion. Mentally wealthy individuals accept themselves, with all their strengths and weaknesses; they practice self-compassion. They treat themselves with kindness, understanding, and forgiveness, embracing imperfections as part of the human experience.

Cognitive flexibility. Cognitive flexibility involves the ability to adapt one's thinking, consider alternative perspectives, and adjust to new information or situations. It includes being open-minded, curious, and willing to learn and grow intellectually.

Lifelong learning. Engaging in continuous learning and intellectual stimulation contributes to mental wealth. It involves seeking knowledge, exploring new interests, and challenging oneself intellectually through activities such as reading, attending educational courses, or engaging in hobbies that promote cognitive growth.

Stress management. Effectively managing stress is essential for mental wealth. It includes developing healthy coping strategies, such as relaxation techniques, mindfulness practices, physical exercise, and seeking social support. Managing stress helps maintain mental well-being and prevents the negative impact of chronic stress.

Healthy relationships. Nurturing healthy and supportive relationships is crucial for mental wealth. Positive social connections provide emotional support, a sense of belonging, and opportunities for growth and personal development.

Purpose and meaning. Having a sense of purpose and meaning is an important aspect of mental wealth. It involves identifying and pursuing meaningful goals, values, and passions that align with one's core beliefs and aspirations. Having a sense of purpose can enhance motivation, satisfaction, and overall mental well-being.

Mindfulness and self-awareness. Practicing mindfulness and developing self-awareness contribute to mental wealth. Mindfulness involves being fully present in the moment, nonjudgmentally observing thoughts and emotions. Self-awareness helps in understanding one's thoughts, emotions, and behaviors, leading to greater self-understanding and personal growth.

Psychological well-being. Mental wealth includes overall psychological well-being, which encompasses factors such as life satisfaction, positive emotions, a sense of autonomy, personal growth, and a sense of control over one's life. Psychological well-being reflects a state of thriving and flourishing in various aspects of life.

Personal Freedom

I've frequently used the term *personal freedom* in this book. What, then, is it?

Personal freedom is the ultimate wealth. It's having the money you need to live the life you want. It's having deep and satisfying relationships with other people. It's being physically and emotionally healthy and having a spiritual connection with something greater than yourself. Personal freedom is about constantly learning and growing and becoming a better version of yourself.

14

The World-Class Life

There you have it. You now have everything you need to take a quantum leap with a new World-Class Wealth Mindset.

The Four Pillars of Success

Image   Standard   Attitude   Discipline

I hope you have been doing the exercises and taking the actions all along and are already starting to see some changes.

You have one life. How are you living it? Are you investing in yourself and your growth? Are you working on raising your Image and Standard and choosing your Attitude? Are you engaging in Discipline every day?

Keep Choosing the World-Class Life

I want you to keep choosing the world-class life. Bet on yourself. Go all in. Choosing to live a world-class life every day is a powerful mindset that can lead to personal growth, success, and fulfillment.

Define what a world-class life means to you. Clearly articulate your goals, values, and aspirations. Visualize the kind of life you want to live and the person you want to become. This clarity will guide your daily choices and actions.

Commit to ongoing learning and personal development. Seek opportunities to expand your knowledge, skills, and perspectives. Stay curious, read books, attend seminars, take courses, and surround yourself with people who inspire and challenge you to grow.

Pursue mastery in your chosen field or passion. Strive for excellence in everything you do. Dedicate time and effort to honing your skills, refining your expertise, and delivering exceptional results. Take pride in your work, and consistently raise the bar for yourself.

Cultivate a positive and empowering mindset. Embrace optimism, resilience, and a belief in your own potential. Practice gratitude, focus on solutions, and maintain a growth-oriented attitude. Surround yourself with positive influences, and minimize exposure to negativity.

Develop discipline in your daily routines and habits. Consistently take actions aligned with your vision and goals. Prioritize your time and energy on behalf of activities that contribute to your personal growth and progress. Stay committed even when faced with challenges or setbacks.

Seek to make a positive impact on others and the world around you. Be of service: share your knowledge, skills, and resources with others. Look for opportunities to contribute to causes that align with your values. Recognize that true success is often measured by the positive difference we make in the lives of others.

Prioritize self-care to maintain physical, mental, and emotional well-being. Take care of your health, engage in activities that bring you joy and relaxation, and nurture positive relationships. Strive for balance and make time for self-reflection and rejuvenation.

Embrace challenges as opportunities for growth. Step outside of your comfort zone, and take calculated risks. Learn from failures and setbacks, using them as stepping stones to further improvement.

Embrace a mindset of continuous improvement; never settle for mediocrity.

Attaining financial freedom is not an overnight accomplishment. It demands time, effort, and investments. Cultivating a vision of success is essential when aiming for financial well-being. This encompasses being mindful of your spending habits and possessing a well-defined financial plan. Steer clear of impulsive purchases; instead develop an investment strategy that aligns with your needs. Educate yourself on different investment opportunities, such as stocks and bonds. Investing in yourself is crucial, because it fosters vital skills like discipline and strategic planning. By adopting healthy financial habits and embodying a successful mindset, you can progress towards financial freedom and secure your future.

Attitude plays a significant role not only in our personal lives but also in our financial pursuits. Maintaining a positive outlook can make the difference between staying motivated during challenging times and succumbing to defeat before even starting. For achieving financial goals, a positive attitude should never be underestimated: it cultivates creativity and enables us to devise innovative solutions to obstacles. Moreover, it safeguards against burnout by keeping us focused on our objectives and determined to succeed, regardless of how arduous the journey may seem.

Mindset Coaching

Your pursuit of personal freedom means more than mere monetary decisions; it also involves envisioning success and cultivating the right attitude. As long as you remain dedicated and resilient, you will achieve your financial goals with ease. Ultimately, it all comes down to believing in yourself and taking control of your financial future. With a focus on meaningful steps and consistent progress, you can achieve the life that suits you best. Hard work always pays off, so keep striving for the life that aligns with your aspirations!

Success does not solely depend on individual skills and knowledge; mindset plays a pivotal role. Carol Dweck, a renowned psychologist and author of *Mindset: The New Psychology of Success*, introduced the groundbreaking concept of the *growth mindset*. It revolutionized psychology by emphasizing that intelligence, talent, and abilities can be developed through hard work, feedback, and continuous learning. As a result, mindset coaching has emerged as an indispensable tool for personal and professional growth in this thriving industry.

What exactly is mindset coaching? It is a specialized form of life coaching that helps you tap into the power of your thoughts, beliefs, and attitudes to unlock your full potential. Its primary objective is to dismantle self-imposed mental barriers and overcome limiting beliefs. Through techniques such as self-reflection, visualization, and reframing of thought patterns, mindset coaches empower you to embrace your true potential by fostering resilience, adaptability, and self-confidence.

Here are five compelling reasons why mindset coaching is a necessity:

1. Accelerated technological advancements. In a rapidly evolving landscape, with advancing technologies and emerging industries, agility, adaptability, and continuous learning have become crucial for professional relevance. A growth mindset allows you to embrace change, dare to experiment, and take calculated risks, fostering innovation and facilitating better decision-making.

2. Fostering emotional intelligence. Mindset coaching cultivates emotional intelligence, enhancing traits such as self-awareness, empathy, and effective communication. This development translates into enhanced teamwork, stronger interpersonal relationships, and improved mental well-being.

3. Combating stress and burnout. The fast-paced and demanding modern lifestyle often leads to chronic stress and burnout. Through the cultivation of mental resilience and coping strategies, mindset coaching empowers you to better manage stress levels and maintain a healthy work-life balance.

4. High competition in the job market. A strong mindset enables you to persevere in the face of adversity, bounce back from failures, and continuously strive for personal growth. These qualities make you more employable, giving you an advantage in a highly competitive job market.

5. Nurturing inclusive workplaces. As diversity, equity, and inclusion initiatives gain prominence in organizations, cultivating a growth mindset becomes instrumental in fostering an open, adaptable, and inclusive work culture. This in turn creates a safer work environment, leading to higher employee satisfaction, productivity, and innovation.

In summary, the mindset coaching industry is rapidly expanding and will continue to grow as mental well-being, adaptability, and resilience gain importance. By engaging with a mindset coach, you can break through personal barriers, overcome challenges, and unlock your true potential so you can thrive personally and professionally.

By consciously choosing the World-Class Mindset every day, you are setting yourself on a path of personal excellence and fulfillment. Embrace the journey, stay committed to your vision, and celebrate the progress you make along the way. Remember that each day presents an opportunity to make choices that align with your highest aspirations and bring you closer to living a world-class life.

15

Vossisms

Below are some aphorisms that I've found helpful personally and in working with my clients.

- Change is difficult in the beginning, gets comfortable in the middle, and it's beautiful at the end!
- Discipline takes you where motivation doesn't.
- Make a committed decision and stop screwing around with yourself.
- To get to the top 1 percent is not hard. All it takes is effort.
- How you start your day is how you own your day.
- You are the only problem you will ever have, and you are the only solution.
- See yourself living in abundance, and you will attract it. It works every time with every person.
- You must do what others won't: commit and stay the course.
- Make a committed decision, and act on it within thirty seconds.
- Success is in our failures.
- Your past has prepared you for greatness.
- No problem outside you is greater than the power within you.
- Faith and fear both require you to believe in something you cannot see. You choose.
- Once you make the decision, you will find all the people, resources, and ideas you need, every time.
- See yourself where you want to be, and then be there.
- Don't be in the past. Be there! Act like the person you want to become.

✤ People who are interested in doing something will do it when it's convenient. People who are committed will do it no matter what.

✤ Do you want to know what you think about most of the time? Take a look at your results. They will tell you exactly what's going on inside.

✤ Thoughts become things. If you see it in your mind, you will hold it in your hand.

APPENDIX

Worksheets and Quizzes

Worksheet 1: The Four-Pillar Pledge

Instructions. This worksheet is designed to help you strengthen the four pillars of the pledge: Image, Standard, Attitude, and Discipline. By focusing on these areas, you can enhance your personal development and create positive changes in your life. Take your time to reflect on each pillar, and complete the exercises. Write down your thoughts, goals, and action steps on your own paper or on your computer.

1. Image
- Reflect on your current self-image and how it aligns with your desired self.
- Write down the qualities, values, and characteristics you want to embody.
- Identify any negative beliefs or self-perceptions that may hinder your self-image.

Action Steps
- Choose one aspect of your self-image you would like to improve.
- Write down affirmations or positive statements that support your desired self-image.
- Commit to practicing daily affirmations and visualizations to reinforce a positive self-image.

2. Standard
- Evaluate your current standards in different areas of your life (such as relationships, career, health).

- Write down your current standards and identify areas where you would like to raise them.
- Consider what actions and behaviors would reflect a higher Standard for you.

Action Steps
- Select one area where you want to raise your Standard.
- Define specific actions or behaviors that align with your desired higher Standard.
- Create a plan and commit to taking consistent action to meet and exceed your new Standard.

3. Attitude
- Reflect on your Attitude and mindset in various situations.
- Identify any negative attitudes or limiting beliefs that hold you back.
- Consider how adopting a positive mental attitude can positively impact your life.

Action Steps
- Choose one negative attitude or limiting belief you want to change.
- Challenge and reframe that belief into a positive, empowering perspective.
- Practice mindfulness and self-awareness to monitor and adjust your attitude in different situations.

4. Discipline
- Assess your level of discipline in pursuing your goals and maintaining healthy habits.
- Identify areas where you need to improve discipline and consistency.

- Consider the actions and habits that contribute to a disciplined lifestyle.

Action Steps
- Select one habit or behavior you want to improve through discipline.
- Define specific actions and routines that support your desired discipline.
- Set realistic goals, and create a plan to establish and reinforce the habit of carrying them out.

Commitment

Commit to embracing and strengthening the four pillars of the pledge: Image, Standard, Attitude, and Discipline. Use this worksheet as a guide to reflect, set goals, and take action towards personal growth and self-improvement. Regularly revisit and reassess your progress to ensure you stay on track. It's through consistent effort and commitment that you can create positive change and live a fulfilling life aligned with your values and aspirations.

Take the Pledge

Worksheet 2: How Has My Past Prepared Me for Greatness?

Instructions. Reflecting on your past experiences and journey can provide valuable insights into how they have shaped you and prepared you for greatness. Use the following prompts and questions to explore and appreciate the ways in which your past has contributed to your personal growth, resilience, and potential for achieving greatness. Take your time to answer the questions honestly and thoughtfully. Write down your responses.

1. Reflection on Challenges
- What significant challenges or obstacles have you faced in your life?
- How did you navigate through these challenges? What strengths or qualities did you draw upon?
- What did you learn about yourself during these challenging times?

2. Lessons Learned
- What valuable life lessons have you gained from your past experiences?
- How have these lessons helped you become wiser, more resilient, or more compassionate?
- How do these lessons contribute to your personal growth and readiness for greatness?

3. Skills and Abilities
- What skills or abilities have you developed over the years?
- How have these skills and abilities served you in various aspects of your life?
- In what ways can you leverage these skills and abilities to achieve greatness?

4. Personal Growth and Transformation
- Reflect on your personal growth journey. How have you evolved as a person over time?
- What positive changes have you experienced in terms of mindset, beliefs, or self-awareness?
- How has this personal growth prepared you for embracing opportunities and pursuing greatness?

5. Resilience and Overcoming Adversity
- Recall moments when you faced setbacks, failures, or adversity.
- How did you bounce back from these challenges and continue moving forward?
- How has your resilience in the face of adversity shaped your character and determination?

6. Relationships and Support
- Reflect on the people who have influenced and supported you throughout your life.
- How have these relationships contributed to your personal development and growth?
- In what ways have these connections prepared you for greatness?

7. Achievements and Milestones

- Celebrate your past achievements and milestones, both big and small.
- How have these accomplishments instilled confidence and a belief in your potential for greatness?
- What can you learn from these achievements and apply to future endeavors?

8. Embracing Your Unique Story

- Embrace your unique life story and the experiences that make you who you are.
- How does your past provide a unique perspective or set of skills that can contribute to your greatness?
- How can you honor and embrace your personal narrative as you strive for greatness?

Reflection and Action Steps

- Review your responses. Appreciate the journey you have been on and the ways in which your past has prepared you for greatness.
- Identify key insights or themes that emerge from your reflections.
- Consider how you can leverage your past experiences, strengths, and lessons learned to propel yourself towards greatness.
- Write down one or two actionable steps you can take based on these insights.
- Commit to taking consistent and focused action to realize your full potential.

Your past does not define your future, but it can serve as a powerful foundation for your journey towards greatness. Embrace the lessons, strengths, and resilience gained from your past, and let them guide you towards a brighter and more fulfilling future.

Worksheet 3:
Design My Life Masterpiece

Instructions. This worksheet is designed to help you envision and create a detailed plan for designing your life masterpiece. Reflect on your aspirations, goals, and desires across various areas of your life. Use the following prompts and questions to guide your thinking and inspire your vision. Write down your responses.

1. Define Your Vision
- What is your ultimate vision for your life? Describe it in vivid detail.
- What does living a fulfilling and meaningful life look like to you?
- What areas of your life do you want to focus on (for example, career, relationships, health, personal growth)?

2. Identify Your Core Values
- What are your core values? These are the guiding principles that shape your decisions and actions.
- How can you align your life with these values to create a sense of fulfillment and authenticity?

3. Set Meaningful Goals
- What specific goals do you want to achieve in the different areas of your life?

- Make your goals *specific*, *measurable*, *attainable*, *relevant*, and *time-bound* (SMART).
- Write down your goals for each area, including career, relationships, health, personal growth, and any other important aspects.

4. Envision Your Ideal Day

- Describe your ideal day from morning to evening.
- How do you spend your time? What activities bring you joy and fulfillment?
- Incorporate elements that align with your goals, values, and aspirations.

5. Create an Action Plan

- Break down each of your goals into smaller, actionable steps.
- Determine the resources, skills, or support you may need to achieve each step.
- Assign deadlines and milestones to keep yourself accountable.

6. Overcome Challenges

- Identify potential obstacles or challenges that may arise on your journey.
- Brainstorm strategies or solutions to overcome these challenges.
- Consider seeking support from mentors, coaches, or friends who can help you stay motivated and focused.

7. Cultivate Positive Habits

- What positive habits or routines can you incorporate into your daily life to support your goals?
- How can you prioritize self-care, personal development, and consistent progress?
- Write down three to five habits that will positively impact your journey towards your life masterpiece.

8. Review and Adjust

- Regularly review your progress and assess if any adjustments or refinements are needed.
- Stay open to new opportunities and experiences that align with your vision.
- Celebrate milestones and achievements along the way.

9. Reflection and Commitment

Review your responses and immerse yourself in the vision you have created for your life masterpiece. Reflect on the excitement, inspiration, and sense of purpose it brings. Make a commitment to yourself to take consistent action towards designing and living your life according to this vision. Set aside regular time to revisit and revise your plan as needed, ensuring it remains aligned with your evolving aspirations and desires.

You have the power to design and create a life that reflects your truest self and brings you immense fulfillment. Embrace this opportunity, and embark on the journey of crafting your own life masterpiece.

Worksheet 4: Mental Attitude Shift

Instructions. This worksheet is designed to help you identify and shift from a negative to a positive mental attitude. It will guide you through self-reflection and practical steps to cultivate a more optimistic and empowering mindset. Take your time to complete each section and be honest with yourself. Use the space provided to write down your responses and action steps.

1. Identify Negative Thought Patterns

- Reflect on the negative thoughts and beliefs that frequently arise in your mind.
- Write down specific examples of negative self-talk or limiting beliefs.
- Be aware of patterns such as self-doubt, criticism, fear, or pessimism.

2. Challenge Negative Thoughts

- Examine the validity of your negative thoughts and beliefs.
- Ask yourself: Is there evidence to support these thoughts? Are they based on facts or assumptions?
- Identify any distortions or irrational thinking that may be contributing to your negative mindset.

3. Reframe Negative Thoughts

- Once you've recognized negative thoughts, reframe them into more positive and empowering statements.
- Write down alternative, realistic, and positive perspectives for each negative thought or belief.
- Focus on affirmations and statements that uplift and motivate you.

4. Practice Gratitude

- Shift your attention towards gratitude and appreciation.
- List three things you are grateful for each day, focusing on both big and small blessings.
- Cultivate a habit of acknowledging and expressing gratitude regularly.

5. Surround Yourself with Positivity

- Evaluate the influence of people, media, and environments on your mindset.
- Identify and eliminate sources that consistently promote negativity.
- Seek out positive and supportive people, inspirational content, and uplifting environments.

6. Engage in Positive Self-Talk

- Monitor your self-talk, and consciously replace negative self-talk with positive affirmations.
- Write down three empowering affirmations that counteract your negative beliefs.
- Repeat these affirmations daily to reinforce a positive mindset.

7. Practice Mindfulness and Self-Awareness
- Cultivate mindfulness to observe your thoughts and emotions without judgment.
- Notice when negative thoughts arise and gently redirect your focus to positive aspects.
- Engage in activities that promote self-awareness, such as meditation or journaling.

8. Take Action and Celebrate Progress
- Set small, achievable goals that align with a positive mindset.
- Take action steps towards these goals, focusing on progress rather than perfection.
- Celebrate each milestone, and acknowledge the growth you've achieved.

9. Seek Support
- Reach out to supportive friends, family, or mentors who can encourage and uplift you.
- Consider working with a coach or therapist to help you navigate your mindset shift.

10. Review and Reflect
- Regularly review your progress and reflect on the changes in your mindset.
- Notice any improvements in your overall well-being, resilience, and positivity.
- Adjust your approach as needed, and continue to prioritize your mental well-being.

Commitment

Commit to implementing the strategies and action steps outlined in this worksheet. Embrace the process of shifting from a negative mental attitude to a positive mental attitude. Be patient with yourself, as change takes time and consistent effort. Remember, you have the power to shape your mindset and create a more empowering and fulfilling life experience.

Worksheet 5: Command Control

Instructions. This worksheet is designed to help you take command of your mind and cultivate discipline in your thought patterns. It will guide you through self-reflection and practical exercises to strengthen your mental control and focus. Take your time to complete each section, and be committed to practicing the strategies consistently. Use the space provided to write down your responses and action steps.

1. Awareness of Thoughts
- Observe your thoughts throughout the day.
- Notice any recurring negative or unhelpful thought patterns.
- Write down specific examples of thoughts that you want to discipline.

2. Identify Limiting Beliefs
- Reflect on any beliefs that hold you back or limit your potential.
- Write down the limiting beliefs that you currently hold.
- Be honest with yourself and identify the impact these beliefs have on your life.

3. Reframe Limiting Beliefs
- Challenge your limiting beliefs and reframe them into empowering beliefs.

- Write down alternative, positive beliefs that support your goals and aspirations.
- Focus on affirmations that counteract your limiting beliefs.

4. Mindful Awareness

- Practice mindfulness to become more aware of your thoughts and emotions.
- Set aside dedicated time each day for mindfulness exercises, such as meditation or deep breathing.
- Notice when negative or distracting thoughts arise, and consciously redirect your focus to positive or productive thoughts.

5. Create Positive Affirmations

- Develop a list of positive affirmations that align with your goals and values.
- Write down affirmations that reinforce discipline, focus, and mental strength.
- Repeat these affirmations daily, especially during challenging moments or when you feel your discipline wavering.

6. Implement Mental Exercises

- Engage in mental exercises to strengthen your focus and discipline.
- Practice activities such as visualization, concentration exercises, or memory games.
- Set aside dedicated time each day to engage in these exercises and gradually increase the difficulty.

7. Establish a Routine
- Create a daily routine that supports mental discipline.
- Schedule specific times for activities that require focused attention, such as reading, learning, or problem-solving.
- Stick to your routine consistently, even and especially on days when motivation is low.

8. Avoid Distractions
- Identify common distractions that hinder your mental discipline.
- Write down specific distractions, whether they are external (e.g., social media) or internal (e.g., self-doubt).
- Develop strategies to minimize or eliminate these distractions from your environment or mindset.

9. Accountability and Tracking
- Hold yourself accountable for your progress in disciplining your mind.
- Set measurable goals related to your mental discipline, such as reducing negative thinking or improving focus during tasks.
- Track your progress regularly and celebrate small victories along the way.

10. Seek Support
- Share your commitment to disciplining your mind with a trusted friend, family member, or mentor.
- Ask for their support and encouragement in holding yourself accountable.

- Consider joining a Mastermind group or seeking guidance from a coach to further strengthen your discipline.

Commitment

Commit to implementing the strategies and exercises outlined in this worksheet. Embrace the process of commanding and disciplining your mind. Be patient with yourself, as developing mental discipline takes time and consistent effort. Remember, you have the power to shape your thoughts and cultivate a focused, disciplined mind that supports your personal and professional growth.

Worksheet 6: Raise Your Self-Image

Instructions. This worksheet is designed to help you raise your self-image and cultivate a positive perception of yourself. It will guide you through self-reflection and practical exercises to boost your self-esteem and confidence. Take your time to complete each section, and be committed to practicing the strategies consistently. Use the space provided to write down your responses and action steps.

1. Self-Reflection

- Reflect on your current self-image and how it affects your life.
- Write down any negative beliefs or self-perceptions that you hold about yourself.
- Identify specific areas where you would like to raise your self-image.

2. Positive Self-Talk

- Become aware of your inner dialogue and replace self-critical thoughts with positive affirmations.
- Write down empowering statements that reflect your strengths, abilities, and unique qualities.
- Practice repeating these affirmations daily to reinforce positive self-talk.

3. Strengths and Achievements

- Identify your strengths, talents, and past achievements.

- Write down a list of accomplishments that you are proud of, both big and small.
- Recognize the skills and qualities that contribute to your success and self-worth.

4. Personal Development
- Set goals for personal growth and development.
- Write down areas of self-improvement that you would like to focus on.
- Create an action plan with specific steps to enhance your skills and knowledge in these areas.

5. Surround Yourself with Positivity
- Evaluate the people and environments that influence your self-image.
- Identify supportive and positive people who uplift and encourage you.
- Minimize contact with negative influences that undermine your self-esteem.

6. Practice Self-Care
- Prioritize self-care activities that nourish your mind, body, and soul.
- Write down self-care practices that make you feel good about yourself, such as exercise, healthy eating, adequate rest, and engaging in hobbies or activities you enjoy.
- Schedule regular self-care routines and commit to them.

7. Visualization

- Use the power of visualization to enhance your self-image.
- Close your eyes and imagine yourself as the best version of yourself.
- Visualize your desired qualities, achievements, and the confident way you carry yourself.

8. Celebrate Small Wins

- Acknowledge and celebrate your accomplishments, no matter how small.
- Write down a list of small wins that you have achieved recently or milestones that you have crossed.
- Take a moment to appreciate your progress and give yourself credit.

9. Affirming Boundaries

- Identify boundaries that are important to your self-worth and well-being.
- Write down specific boundaries that you want to establish or reinforce in your relationships and personal life.
- Practice communicating and upholding these boundaries assertively and respectfully.

10. Gratitude Practice

- Cultivate gratitude for yourself and your journey.
- Write down things you are grateful for about yourself, your experiences, and your growth.
- Take time each day to express gratitude for the positive aspects of your life.

Commitment

Commit to implementing the strategies and exercises outlined in this worksheet. Embrace the process of raising your self-image and developing a positive perception of yourself. Be patient with yourself, as building a healthy self-image takes time and consistent effort. Remember, you are deserving of love, respect, and confidence. Believe in your worth, and let it shine through in all aspects of your life.

Quiz: What's in My Subconscious?

Circle the statements that apply to you. Do this quickly, without thinking too much about your response. Circle the ones that might apply even if you're not sure.

1. I find it hard to ask for what I am worth financially.
2. I have negative feelings about or am envious of wealthy people.
3. Someone else outside of me is responsible for my financial situation.
4. I am proud of my ability to get the best price on things.
5. I have a family history of debt or financial problems.
6. I keep trying to make more money but never seem to be able to break through.
7. I am good at managing money, but there's never enough to go around.
8. It takes hard work and a lot of hours to become wealthy.
9. I feel I'm never going to be able to achieve my financial goals.
10. No matter how much I achieve, I'm always looking for the next goal.
11. I love money and what it can do for my life.
12. I believe I can change my financial future.
13. I am willing to take consistent action to achieve my goals.
14. I am passionate about my work.
15. There are some wealthy people that I consider to be role models or mentors.
16. I have no problem asking to be paid what I am worth.
17. I feel grateful most of the time for the life I am living.

18. Every day I am getting better than I was the day before.
19. I am tenacious and disciplined in achieving the goals I want to achieve.
20. No one can hold me back from my dreams.

Scoring

If you circled more of questions 1–10, your subconscious mind has received some negative programming that is likely affecting your financial abundance. If you circled more questions 11–20, you are likely already experiencing wealth and are ready to learn to take it to the next level.

The Relationship with Money Quiz

This quiz will help you gain insights into your current beliefs, attitudes, and behaviors related to money. Answer each question honestly. At the end, you will receive your quiz results along with some suggestions for improving your relationship with money.

1. How do you feel when you think about money?
   a. Excited and confident
   b. Anxious and stressed
   c. Indifferent and neutral
   d. Unsure and confused

2. How do you approach financial decisions?
   a. I carefully plan and consider all options.
   b. I tend to avoid making financial decisions.
   c. I make impulsive decisions based on emotions.
   d. I rely on others to make financial decisions for me.

3. How do you view wealth and abundance?
   a. I believe there are unlimited opportunities for wealth.
   b. I feel that wealth is reserved for a select few.
   c. I think wealth is not important in life.
   d. I'm not sure how to achieve wealth and abundance.

4. How do you handle financial setbacks or challenges?
   a. I see them as opportunities for growth and learning.
   b. I feel overwhelmed and discouraged.
   c. I ignore them and hope they will resolve themselves.
   d. I rely on others to help me navigate through them.

5. How do you prioritize saving and investing?
    a. I make it a top priority and consistently save and invest.
    b. I struggle to save and invest regularly.
    c. I haven't thought much about saving and investing.
    d. I leave it to chance and don't have a clear plan.

6. How do you feel about spending money on yourself?
    a. I believe it's important to invest in my own well-being.
    b. I feel guilty or selfish when I spend money on myself.
    c. I rarely spend money on myself; I prioritize others.
    d. I'm unsure about the balance between spending on myself and others.

7. How do you talk about money with others?
    a. I am open and comfortable discussing money matters.
    b. I avoid discussing money; it makes me uncomfortable.
    c. Money is not a topic of conversation for me.
    d. I rely on others to handle money discussions.

8. How do you define financial success?
    a. Having financial freedom and security.
    b. Accumulating material possessions and wealth.
    c. Not worrying about money and living a simple life.
    d. I'm not sure what financial success means to me.

Scoring

Now tally up your answers and find out your quiz results!

Mostly A's. Congratulations! You have a positive and healthy relationship with money. You are proactive, financially responsible, and have a growth mindset when it comes to wealth. Keep up the good work and continue to build on your financial success.

Mostly B's. Your relationship with money may be causing stress and anxiety. It's essential to examine your beliefs and attitudes towards money and work on developing a more positive mindset. Seek financial education and resources to improve your financial confidence and decision-making skills.

Mostly C's. Money may not be a significant focus for you, but it's essential to understand its role in your life. Consider exploring your financial goals and how money can support your overall well-being and future aspirations. Developing a healthy relationship with money can bring more stability and freedom.

Mostly D's. It seems that you have some uncertainties and confusion regarding money. It's crucial to educate yourself, seek guidance, and clarify your financial goals. Developing a clear understanding of money management and adopting positive financial habits can lead to a healthier relationship with money.

This quiz provides general insights. It's always beneficial to consult with financial professionals for personalized advice. Use the results as a starting point for self-reflection and growth in your relationship with money.

The Discipline Quiz

What can you do with an unwavering level of discipline? How would your life look and what could you achieve?

Instructions. Read each question and choose the option that best represents your response. At the end of the quiz, you will receive your results indicating the potential outcomes of having an unwavering level of discipline in your life.

1. How do you typically approach tasks or projects?
   a. I often procrastinate and struggle to stay focused.
   b. I start with enthusiasm but lose momentum along the way.
   c. I consistently stay committed and follow through until completion.

2. How do you handle distractions or temptations that arise while working towards a goal?
   a. I easily give in to distractions and lose track of my priorities.
   b. I occasionally get sidetracked but can refocus after some time.
   c. I am highly disciplined and can resist distractions to stay on track.

3. How consistent are you in maintaining daily habits or routines?
   a. I frequently break my habits or routines and struggle with consistency.

b. I can be consistent for a while, but then I lose motivation and fall off track.

c. I am dedicated to my daily habits and routines, rarely deviating from them.

4. How do you handle setbacks or obstacles that come your way?

a. I often get discouraged and give up easily when faced with challenges.

b. I may feel temporarily discouraged but can bounce back with effort.

c. I persevere through setbacks and use them as opportunities for growth.

5. How do you prioritize your time and manage your schedule?

a. I struggle to prioritize effectively and often feel overwhelmed.

b. I have some level of organization but find it challenging to stick to my schedule.

c. I have a clear system for prioritizing tasks and managing my time effectively.

6. How do you approach long-term goals or projects?

a. I tend to lose interest or motivation before I can achieve significant progress.

b. I make progress but often get sidetracked or abandon goals halfway through.

c. I maintain focus and work diligently until I accomplish my long-term goals.

7. How do you respond to commitments or obligations you have made to others?
   a. I frequently struggle to meet commitments and may disappoint others.
   b. I make an effort to fulfill my commitments but occasionally fall short.
   c. I consistently follow through on my commitments and can be relied upon.

8. How well do you manage your finances and save money?
   a. I struggle with financial discipline and often overspend or live beyond my means.
   b. I make some attempts to save money but find it challenging to be consistent.
   c. I am disciplined in managing my finances, saving regularly, and living within my means.

Scoring

Now tally up your answers and find out your quiz results.

Mostly A's. Developing a higher level of discipline could greatly transform your life. With unwavering discipline, you can overcome challenges, stay focused on your goals, and achieve remarkable success. Cultivating discipline will require dedicated effort and a commitment to personal growth.

Mostly B's. You have some level of discipline, but there is room for improvement. With a stronger commitment to discipline, you can elevate your achievements and experience greater fulfillment. Focus on building consistent habits and overcoming obstacles to reach your full potential.

Mostly C's. Congratulations! You already possess a high level of discipline, which greatly contributes to your success and personal growth. Your disciplined approach allows you to stay focused, persevere through challenges, and achieve remarkable outcomes. Continue nurturing and harnessing your discipline to reach even greater heights.

This quiz is designed for entertainment and self-reflection purposes. The results are not definitive assessments of your level of discipline but can provide insights

Quiz: Is Your Belief System Holding You Back?

1. How often do you catch yourself thinking negatively about your abilities or potential?
   a. Rarely or never
   b. Occasionally
   c. Frequently

2. When you are faced with a new challenge, what is your immediate reaction?
   a. I see it as an opportunity for growth and success.
   b. I feel uncertain and doubt my ability to handle it.
   c. I assume I won't be able to overcome it.

3. Do you believe that you have the power to change your circumstances and create the life you desire?
   a. Absolutely; I believe in my ability to shape my reality.
   b. I'm not sure, but I hope it's possible
   c. No, I believe external factors determine my outcomes

4. How often do you compare yourself to others and feel inadequate?
   a Rarely or never
   b. Occasionally
   c. Frequently

5. When facing setbacks or failures, how do you interpret
    them?
    a. I see them as valuable learning experiences and
       opportunities to improve.
    b. I tend to blame myself and feel discouraged.
    c. I see them as proof that I'm not capable of succeeding.

6. How much do you believe in your own potential for
    growth and development?
    a. I strongly believe in my capacity to grow and learn.
    b. I have some doubts, but I'm open to the idea of
       personal growth.
    c. I doubt my ability to change or improve significantly.

7. How often do you take risks or step outside of your
    comfort zone?
    a. Frequently; I believe that growth happens outside of
       comfort zones.
    b. Occasionally, but I often hesitate or feel apprehensive.
    c. Rarely; I prefer to stay within my comfort zone

8. Do you believe that failure is an essential part of the
    learning and growth process?
    a. Yes, I embrace failure as a stepping stone to success.
    b. I'm not sure, but I try to learn from my failures.
    c. No, I see failure as a sign of personal inadequacy.

9. How much influence do you think your mindset has on
    your overall success and happiness?
    a. A significant amount, I believe mindset is a key
       determinant of success.
    b. I think mindset plays a role, but it's not the sole factor.
    c. I don't believe mindset has much impact on outcomes.

10. Are you open to challenging and questioning your existing beliefs?
    a. Absolutely; I actively seek new perspectives and challenge my beliefs.
    b. I'm open to it, but I sometimes struggle with letting go of old beliefs.
    c. No, I'm resistant to changing my beliefs and prefer to stick to what I already know.

Scoring

Calculate the number of times you selected each option:

Mostly A's. Your belief system is generally empowering and supportive of your growth. You have a positive mindset that propels you forward and allows you to overcome challenges effectively.

Mostly B's. Your belief system may have some limitations or doubts that can hold you back at times. Consider exploring and challenging these beliefs to unlock your full potential.

Mostly C's. Your belief system appears to be holding you back from reaching your full potential. It's important to examine and challenge these limiting beliefs to create a more empowering and supportive belief system.

Beliefs can be changed and reshaped with conscious effort and self-reflection. Embrace the opportunity to explore new beliefs that align with your goals and aspirations, and always remember that you have the power to shape your own reality.

About the Author

ARASH VOSSOUGHI is the cofounder and president of Voss Coaching Co., a company committed to helping professionals and entrepreneurs break through barriers and achieve personal freedom.

As the creator of the Millionaire Mastermind and cohost of the Seven-Figure Standard Podcast, Arash has inspired individuals worldwide to achieve new levels of confidence, discipline, leadership, and revenue. Thanks to his dynamic and engaging communication style, he is highly sought after to speak to the lives of professional athletes and CEOs.